# BIG GAME OF
# NORTH AMERICA

*Text by Erwin A. Bauer*
*Photographs by Erwin and Peggy Bauer*

Voyageur Press

Text copyright © 1997 by Erwin A. Bauer
Photographs copyright © 1997 by Erwin Bauer and Peggy Bauer

Edited by Michael Dregni
Designed by Leslie Ross
Printed in Hong Kong

98  99  00  01  02  5  4  3  2  1

**Library of Congress Cataloging-in-Publication Data**
Bauer, Erwin A.
    Big game of North America / text by Erwin A. Bauer ; photography
by Erwin and Peggy Bauer.
        p.    cm.
    Includes bibliographical references (p. 155) and index.
    ISBN 0-89658-336-8
    1.  Big game animals—North America.   2.  Mammals—North America.
I. Bauer, Peggy.  II. Title.
QL715.B28   1997
599.097—dc20                                                    96-35224
                                                                CIP

Distributed in Canada by Raincoast Books, 8680 Cambie Street, Vancouver, B.C. V6P 6M9

Published by Voyageur Press, Inc.
123 North Second Street, P.O. Box 338, Stillwater, MN 55082 U.S.A.
612-430-2210, fax 612-430-2211

*Please write or call, or stop by, for our free catalog of natural history publications.*
Our toll-free number to place an order or to obtain a free catalog is 800-888-WOLF (800-888-9653).

*Educators, fundraisers, premium and gift buyers, publicists, and marketing managers:*
Looking for creative products and new sales ideas? Voyageur Press books are available at special
discounts when purchased in quantities, and special editions can be created to your specifications.
For details contact the marketing department.

*Page 1:* September in the Rocky Mountains is an exciting time as bull elk emerge into the high meadows, bugle, fight, gather
harems, and breed. *Page 3:* Cougars are as active in winter as in summer, often hunting in deer and elk wintering ranges. *Page 4:*
Of all North American big game, mountain goats seek out the loftiest, windiest, most precipitous places to spend their lives.

# CONTENTS

# BIG GAME ANIMALS OF NORTH AMERICA

Since the dawn of history, humans have been fascinated by what we today call big game animals. Humans once depended on these animals for survival: Deer, wild sheep, and bears were the source of meat, clothing, shelter, and the first primitive tools. Big game trophies—the heads, hides, horns, and antlers of the largest animals—carried bragging rights even then, just as they do today. From the prehistoric sketches and paintings found on the walls of caves and remote canyons, we surmise that an ancient hunter's standing in his or her tribe greatly depended on the trophies obtained. To some extent this is still true as the twentieth century comes to an end, although more and more people now are thrilled just to watch, study, and photograph wildlife around the world. The more of us that come to respect and care for the future of big game animals, the better the chance that all wild creatures will survive another hundred years.

All North American big game species are mammals. Mammals differ from all other animals in two ways: They grow and are protected by a covering of true hair or fur, and they produce milk with which to feed their young. The hair holds body heat and protects the animal from rain and snow, great heat and intense cold, and from all the crags, stones, and thorns in their environment. Many grow a warmer winter coat of hair or fur each autumn, then shed it every spring for a lighter summer coat.

Compared to many smaller mammals as well as to birds, reptiles, and fish, the coloring of most big game is somber. Depending on whether the animals live out in the open or in forests, hair colors range from tan to dark brown or black—although there is one exception to that rule, in the black-spotted yellow jaguar. The young of many big game species, from deer and elk fawns to cougar kittens, are also spotted, but the spots disappear well before the young are one year old.

*A Montana cougar emerges from forest shadows long enough to drink in a mountain pond. Cougars are shy and seldom seen.*

Young of the carnivorous big game, the bears and cats, are helpless at birth and require a long period of mothering to reach adulthood. But their future victims, the young of hoofed mammals, are able to follow their mothers anywhere within days, if not hours, after entering the world. Hoofed mothers nurse their young standing up; carnivores nurse while lying down.

None of our big game species are picky eaters. By both browsing and grazing, the hoofed animals consume many thousands of different kinds of vegetation—more plants, in fact, than scientists have yet documented. Deer and elk have also been observed (albeit rarely) eating fish and small mammals. Nor are the carnivores selective. The bears will eat anything from grass and grasshoppers to carrion and fresh meat, roots, mushrooms, and berries. The cats will eat any creature they can catch. Finding food and eating it takes up a great part of every big game animal's life.

All North American big game animals are promiscuous, and the males play no part whatever in raising, feeding, or caring for young; females handle all of that. While the ungulates band together much of the year, the carnivores (except females with young) usually go their own way. Some of the hoofed animals migrate great distances every year, caribou laterally for hundreds of miles and elk "vertically" from high summer range to lower winter range and back again. Bears spend the winter in hibernation. All the rest tough it out.

## A Dedication to Saving Big Game

We have not always respected or realized the immense value of North America's big game. In fact, the supply has always seemed inexhaustible. The biggest animals, far more confiding than they are today, were the first to be eliminated by colonists. Hungry for agricultural land, the new arrivals from Europe on both the Atlantic and Pacific shores proceeded with religious zeal to destroy the wilderness they found. Remotely dangerous or competitive creatures had to go, even though Native Americans had lived with the deer and bears for centuries.

The story of the buffalo annihilation on the Great Plains in the late 1800s is well known. But systematic slaughters were taking place long before that. On the Pacific Coast, colonists were eliminating the greatest density of grizzly bears on earth, as well as the once-abundant tule elk. On the Pennsylvania frontier in 1760, one Black Jack Schwartz, known locally as the Wild Hunter, organized a great game drive. According to a witness and reporter of the event, Colonel H. W. Shoemaker, a great gathering of settlers massacred "41 panthers [mountain lions, or cougars], 109 wolves, 17 black bears, 98 deer, 111 buffaloes, 12 gluttons [wolverines] and upwards of 500 smaller mammals." According to Shoemaker: "The choicest hides were taken, together with the buffalo tongues, and then the heap of carcasses as tall as the trees was heaped with rich pine and fired. This created such a stench that the settlers were compelled to vacate their cabins near the fort. There remains a black heap, which on being dug into, is all bones." It sounds ghastly, but the rapid expansion of our civilization today accomplishes the same end, although without the obvious blood and gore.

Today, in the late 1990s, it is the politicians—the men and women we insist on electing to high office—who, with legislation rather than guns, would wipe out our big game. This new approach is far more insidious and effective than the obvious, unregulated attack with firearms. They propose eliminating the Endangered Species Act, opening up our wildlife refuges to all manner of exploitation, and permitting logging roads to divide fatally the previously roadless, primitive areas. In fact, many would give away or sell most of our public lands and wildlife sanctuaries to private, commercial interests. They must be stopped.

This book is dedicated to all citizens and conservation organizations that realize that North America's big game is as precious and worth saving as all the shrines and monuments built by humans. I hope this book will reinforce their thinking and inspire them to work still harder to save our remaining wild places.

*Above:* The Alaskan moose is the largest of all the world's antlered animals. This one in Denali National Park is ready for the rutting season. *Left:* Always wary and alert, a whitetail buck pauses to study the trail ahead through the dense northern evergreen forest that it shares with wolves.

# BIGHORN SHEEP

## *The Sheep with a Crown of Horns*

During summers in the 1980s, hikers and backpackers in the Eagle Cap Wilderness Area of Oregon's Wallowa Mountains reported seeing a huge bighorn ram along the steepest, highest trails. Some called this animal Spot because of the light shading they saw on its chest; others called it Scarface for an old, healed wound between its eyes. For a long time the animal seemed to be a myth, but then someone managed to photograph it while it was on its low-altitude winter range.

When the photograph was published, it caused a sensation among outdoors people: The full-curl horns seemed even heavier than hikers had claimed. When Oregon opened a sheep hunting season in the area, hundreds of trophy hunters applied for permits. But as far as anyone knows, not one of the six permit-holders every fall for nine seasons ever even obtained a glimpse of old Scarface. Some people began to wonder if the photograph was a fake and Scarface a hoax.

The matter was settled in the summer of 1987 when a hiker found the massive ram that had roamed the Eagle Cap Wilderness for fifteen years. Scarface lay where he had died, nearly hidden behind a tumble of large rocks. The hiker removed the horns and turned them over to Vic Coggins, an Oregon Department of Fish and Wildlife biologist. When the horns were measured using the Boone and Crockett Club scoring system, they proved to be the largest known for a bighorn sheep in the United States. Only four other rams have ever scored higher and all of these came from Canada.

In one way, Scarface also belonged to Canada. His father was transplanted by federal biologists from Jasper National Park, Canada, to Oregon in 1971, and he was among the first lambs born there in the Wallowas the following spring. His death fifteen years later may also be a record since no other wild bighorn rams are definitely known to have reached that great age.

*Many consider the North American bighorn sheep the greatest big game animal on earth—and with good cause. The heavy horns of this ram are true trophy size.*

What caused Scarface's death is not nearly as great a mystery as how he eluded serious hunters over the years. Biologists believe the ram died from bacterial pneumonia spread by domestic sheep that the U.S. Forest Service allowed to roam and graze in the area. Soon as many as 110 more sheep in this herd were similarly decimated. Only about thirty-three survived.

The sad story of Scarface's band of sheep tells us a good bit about the bighorn species and how we will manage, or should manage, them for the future. Here is a magnificent dweller of our most remote mountain ranges that on the one hand tolerates and is not too shy of people. But it is also a quick learner. Wherever and whenever hunting seasons open, bighorns suddenly exhibit an uncanny ability to avoid people with rifles and to stay well out of sight. There are plenty of sportspeople who regard the bighorn as the most challenging big game of all, bar none.

It is well known that domestic sheep easily transfer disease that is often fatal to their wild siblings. Therefore, it seems especially strange, even tragic, that conservation officials would allow domestic animals access to an area inhabited by such a splendid native species that is no longer abundant anywhere on the continent. Maybe the case of Scarface will teach a lesson to all of us who love the wild creatures and their environment.

## The "True" American Sheep

The bighorn, *Ovis canadensis*, is one of two North American and several Eurasian wild sheep that belong to the genus, *Ovis*, of true sheep. The other North American species is *Ovis dalli*, the white sheep, or Dall sheep.

A century ago, scientists used every minor variation in size, color, and geographical distribution to separate North American wild sheep into as many as eighteen different classes or subspecies. Today there is consensus that there are only two: the northern bighorn, or Rocky Mountain bighorn, *Ovis canadensis canadensis*, of Wyoming northward to Alberta and British Columbia; and the desert bighorn sheep, *Ovis canadensis nelsoni* and/or *Ovis canadensis mexicana*, with scattered populations in dry mountain habitat of the American Southwest and northern Mexico, including Baja California.

Our only memento of another possible subspecies that has been extinct since 1924 is the full mount of an Audubon bighorn ram that stands in the lobby of the state office building in Pierre, South Dakota. It probably was killed in 1900 by the famous Indian agent

### Range of the Bighorn Sheep (*Ovis canadensis*)

*Note that bighorn sheep today occupy only scattered mountain islands in this range.*

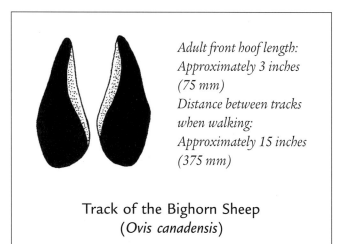

*Adult front hoof length: Approximately 3 inches (75 mm)*
*Distance between tracks when walking: Approximately 15 inches (375 mm)*

### Track of the Bighorn Sheep (*Ovis canadensis*)

Major James McLaughlin near Standing Rock, South Dakota. Audubon bighorns were once widespread in the rugged badlands of eastern Montana, Wyoming, Nebraska, and the Dakotas. As many as one thousand may still have survived when the Pierre ram was shot and skinned.

Traders, trappers, and early explorers found bighorns fairly abundant throughout the Rocky Mountain region in the early nineteenth century. Wintering in 1832 along the Salmon River in what would become

*Male and female bighorns gather on a mountainside in northern Alberta preparing to begin the active, breeding season.*

Idaho, Captain Benjamin Bonneville found both elk and sheep plentiful, but his party preferred and subsisted on sheep because it was easy "to surround and kill as many as we please," and because the meat of the younger ones was the best available, "superior to the finest mutton." Unlike too many other former haunts where sheep are now absent, bighorns still live in the precipices along the Salmon River of No Return, where Peggy and I have spotted them during summertime float trips as they watched us from high above or drank from the water's edge.

We have also watched and photographed bighorns, many not far from our home on the edge of the Absaroka-Beartooth Wilderness Area in Montana. As wild species go, they are fairly predictable, as least until the local hunting season opens.

Viewed up close, bighorns are much larger and more powerful animals than they appear to be when standing on a distant mountainside. Mature rams stand thirty-eight to forty-two inches (95–105 cm) at the shoulder, are broad across the back, and weigh up to 300 pounds (135 kg). Females might measure thirty-

six inches (90 cm) at the shoulder and weigh 150 pounds (67½ kg). All are far more agile and fast afoot over the steepest, most difficult terrain than seems possible for their stocky physiques.

At least two of sheep's senses—their sight and hearing—are keen, probably beyond human comprehension. I do not know if their sense of smell is especially good or not. But the slightest movement on distant alpine ridges immediately is spotted by rams that appeared at first to be dozing and inattentive. The sounds of other species grazing or of small pebbles dislodged along thin game trails warn sheep of interlopers they cannot yet see. Several times through a spotting scope from a great distance, I have watched bands of rams move to another mountain as soon as they heard unseen human climbers that approached from far below.

## The Crown of Horns

Both males and females of all wild sheep have horns composed of a substance called keratin, which is similar to the material in animal hooves, bear claws, and human fingernails. Unlike the antlers of the world's

13

deer, horns are not shed annually, but grow as long as the animal lives and is healthy. On females, the horns are modest, slow growing, and like a goat's in that they are short and slightly curving. Rams' horns are more massive, curling, and spiraling; they sometimes are tightly wound and sometimes spread outward, depending on an individual's genetic background.

The greatest horn development on any of the world's sheep occurs in the Marco Polo sheep males of central Asia's Pamir Range. These rams boast horns that frequently exceed fifty inches (125 cm) long when measured around the outside curve, and where seventy-inch (175-cm) measurements are not unknown. By contrast, only the largest bighorn rams have curls measuring more than forty inches (100 cm).

From spring until fall, when the most nutritious food is available, horn growth is steady and comparatively fast. From fall through winter, growth is retarded, probably due to body chemistry changes during the rut and winter food shortages; these stresses cause the sheep to use up body fat stored during the summer. The annual fall-winter hiatus in horn growth produces a pattern of growth rings around the horn that are similar to the telltale growth rings of a tree trunk. The exact age of a bighorn ram can be determined by counting the number of these rings visible from the base of the horn to its tip.

The largest northern bighorn trophies are taken almost without close competition in Alberta, where eight of the ten largest ram heads were collected, as listed in the *1993 Boone and Crockett Club Records of North American Big Game*. Most of the biggest desert bighorns live in Baja California, Mexico. The largest of these was a head picked up in the desolate Sierra Madre by a Native American in 1940. The number two desert sheep came from Pima County, Arizona.

## Sheep Through the Seasons

Most of the year, bighorns live in two segregated societies. Ewes and lambs, plus a few immature males, form the larger groups that gradually move from low winter ranges to high summer ranges and back again over the course of a year. One old dominant ewe seems to determine when the group will move on and what route

*Throughout most of the year, bighorns such as this one spotted in Glacier National Park, Montana, live in scenes of immense beauty where they are difficult to approach.*

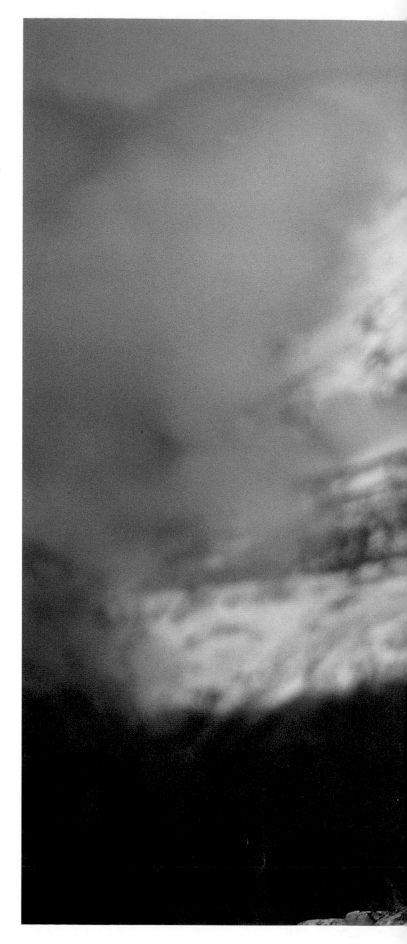

*Bighorn lambs must be agile and able to follow mothers soon after birth. This is the first fall for these young twins near Jasper, Alberta.*

*In ritualized tournaments, bighorn rams fight noisy head-to-head battles to determine which are the strongest and will do most of the breeding.*

they will follow. For example, when late autumn's deepening snows gradually extend farther down the mountainsides and cover food supplies, the dominant ewe will lead the animals to lower elevations or to exposed ridges where strong winds prevent snows from accumulating. Here, they can feed on forage that is still exposed.

Male bighorn societies are smaller and composed of mature bachelors that usually, but not always, live at higher elevations than the females. Their summers are devoted almost entirely to eating and sleeping so they can store up fat and energy for the lean months to come. Then suddenly in fall, the rams are motivated more by the oncoming rut or breeding season than by

coming snows or any other factor. By late fall, rams are never far from the ewes.

The rutting ritual of bighorn sheep must rank with the most exciting spectacles in nature. It usually takes place on the same traditional rutting grounds that the resident herds have used for centuries. In Montana, the rut is well underway by the end of November and may last two weeks. It begins with a tournament of rams in which the younger individuals gradually are eliminated from the breeding process. One or a few—depending on herd size—of the most powerful, dominant rams with the heaviest horns emerge from among all the challengers to do most of the breeding.

Peggy and I often climb to one high meadow overlooking the Gardiner River in Yellowstone Park to watch the annual bighorn bout. It begins sporadically as small bands of rams arrive on the scene from summering grounds, spoiling for action. One morning we counted fifteen rams in a single meadow. Groups of four or five stand close together and each kicks the flank of his neighbor with a swift upward movement of a front leg. This is followed by sniffing, maneuvering, regrouping, and occasional mounting as a sign of dominance.

Eventually the contest boils down to combat between large males of similar size. Two posturing rams will back away, each tipping his head this way and that to show the opponent the size of his horns. Then on some imperceptible signal they stop for a second and stand on hind legs. Finally the two launch into a head-on charge toward one another, their legs driving them as hard as possible. This pile-driving smash might be repeated over and over until one ram concedes by walking or staggering away. Each impact has an explosive sound that echoes like artillery into the foothills where ewes are grazing, paying little attention to the drama unfolding nearby.

We have watched slow-motion footage of clashing bighorns, and it reveals details we could never catch with our own still cameras. The shock from the horn impact actually ripples through the battlers' bodies. Dust, saliva, and horn splinters fly. Blood sometimes drains from eyes and noses, and occasionally both contestants reel drunkenly from the pounding that might last as long as an hour or more. The majority of the bouts we have seen, however, were settled after four or five collisions. From the sidelines, this pre-rut battling is a violent scene.

Although sheep rarely are dangerous to people, there have been a number of serious incidents during the free-for-all rut. Alberta photographer Dave Crosley was pushed off a ledge by an annoyed ram and suffered serious injuries. While studying desert bighorns in California's Sierra Nevada, Illinois student Bob Oprondeck and a colleague were charged by two rams after a steep rock climb. Oprondeck suffered a broken arm among other injuries, but managed to make a twenty-hour march in 100° Fahrenheit (37.7° Celsius) heat with little water to reach medical assistance.

Most fighting is finished and the dominance question settled by the time the first ewe comes into estrus. She is suddenly very popular with the winner or winners of the earlier ram contests. What follows is almost as exciting as the fighting. As they become ready to mate, the ewes are followed relentlessly in high-speed chases, even around the faces of steep precipices. Occasionally one stumbles or starts a small avalanche of rocks and stones. A harried female may try to hide or elude her pursuers by backing into a narrow crevice. But escape is never easy.

Most of the breeding ends by Christmas, and all the bighorns, somewhat exhausted, then are faced with surviving the cold winter and the scanty rations ahead.

The system works. Although weaker or older herd members may not live to enjoy the arrival of spring, all of the surviving females have lambs at about the time the nutritious green vegetation again covers the mountainsides, or about six months after the rut. Soon after birth the lambs are agile and sure-footed enough to follow their mothers anywhere. They spend summers playing and gamboling with other young in the female herd. By the next rutting season, they will be more than half grown.

## The Desert Bighorn Sheep

The desert bighorn sheep is perhaps an even more remarkable creature and survivor than the Rocky Mountain subspecies that I know best. Among the world's larger mammals, it is believed that only the Saharan dromedary camel can surpass the desert bighorn's ability to withstand serious dehydration plus intense heat. Once in Death Valley National Monument, California, we watched thin rams arrive dull-eyed and emaciated at a water seep, seemingly near death. But after slurping the seep almost dry until their stomachs were bulging and following a brief rest in the shade, their vitality was remarkably restored.

Biologists in Death Valley once watched a ram chasing a female at high speed on a day when the official temperature was 122° F (50° C). On another occasion there, two rams were seen fighting near a waterhole for almost two hours non stop, with no sign of fatigue. The temperature that day was 113° F (45° C).

Despite their tenacity, desert bighorns are the most vulnerable of North American sheep. Poaching for trophies has taken a toll, but not nearly so much as loss of habitat and encroachment on bighorn country by domestic livestock. Long periods without rain are a factor as well because even this hardy species can die of thirst. In 1969, California conservation workers found a sheep death trap that had claimed thirty-four animals in the bone-dry Chocolate Mountains. The

animals were lured into a natural rock pit ten feet (3 meters) deep that held runoff water from a desert cloudburst. After drinking, the animals couldn't climb out of the pit. With the help of a U.S. Marine Corps helicopter, an escape route was later blasted into the pit trap to prevent similar tragedies.

Recently, bighorn sheep have been credited with "saving" the small town of Dubois, Wyoming. Located on a main auto route into Yellowstone and Grand Teton National Parks, Dubois had long been a logging and lumbering center until the local sawmill closed in 1988. The community seemed to be dying until local leaders realized that a natural treasure existed not far beyond town limits. The vicinity of Whiskey Mountain had long been the home of about 1,200 bighorns that could easily be seen by passing travelers taking a short detour. Some had always come, but with publicity many more tourists were encouraged to stop and view the sheep. The fine National Bighorn Sheep Interpretive Center opened in 1993. It offered guided day-long trips into bighorn summer habitat for the 21,000 visitors during its first year. That number has been increasing.

Like all the big game of North America, the bighorn sheep are certainly worth saving—by law, by education, by exhibits, by any legal means that we can think of.

*Above:* Desert bighorns like this fine male live in the dry, often hot mountains of the southwestern reaches of the United States, but in smaller numbers than a century ago. ***Right:*** On a high, open meadow early in the rut, bighorn rams posture as the first step to establishing dominance in the herd.

# DALL SHEEP

## *The White Sheep of the Far North*

Throughout the brief, cool summer, travelers driving the Alaska Highway as it passes through Yukon might suddenly come upon an uncommon, handsome animal in the wilderness of Canada's Kluane National Park. The creatures staring down at you from steep rocky slopes along the winding road are Dall sheep, or white sheep, *Ovis dalli dalli*, close cousins of the Rocky Mountain bighorns.

Of all the world's wild sheep, the Dall is the only pure white one. Against the green mountains of summer, or standing on the multi-colored slopes of autumn, the animals are easily spotted from far away. That can be a disadvantage where many predators roam. One springtime in Yukon's Kluane Park, we watched a grizzly bear crisscrossing the meadows above us in a hunt for newborn white lambs. Bears here may be the most important cause of lamb mortality. Once snow covers the land, Dalls become as difficult to see as they were visible six months earlier.

Like most wild sheep, this one thrives best in remote places where there is a mosaic of open alpine ridges and meadows with steep slopes, gorges, or other rugged escape terrain always nearby. The feeding and loafing areas of Dalls must always be within easy reach of sanctuary from predators, especially wolves.

Dall sheep country today includes most of the high mountain ranges of Alaska, Yukon, northern British Columbia, and a western edge of the Mackenzie District, Northwest Territory. Alaska's Brooks Range is the northern limit of the species. Human encroachment into white sheep country has been much less than into the original bighorn range.

*A handsome Dall sheep ram looks out over the lonely Kluane Country in Canada's Yukon. This is the only pure-white species of wild sheep in the world.*

While I have often watched bighorns venturing cautiously down into evergreen forests to feed or visit mineral licks, Dalls almost never come below timberline, except when a band may migrate quickly from one mountain range to another because of food shortages or population pressure. The white sheep are never more vulnerable than during these treks.

I have hunted Dalls with both gun and camera. Hunting with a camera has been much more difficult, and except for spring in Alaska's Denali National Park, it has always required plenty of climbing. Like bighorn rams, Dall males segregate into summer bachelor groups and retreat to the highest elevation where there is enough new green grass, mosses, forbs, and lichens to sustain them. The sheep must accumulate enough body fat from June through September to survive on for the rest of the year. Exactly how they do this is mysterious; time and again I have photographed the rams, sleek and apparently healthy, living on a landscape where none of the vegetation is more than a few inches high and in some places appears to be lacking entirely.

The lifestyles of white sheep are similar to those of bighorns. Where they are not hunted and in national parks where humans are only a part of the environment, they become surprisingly confiding. One morning in Denali, I began the long climb toward the summit of Primrose Mountain, a well-known sheep haunt. The load of camera gear in my backpack was heavy, no sheep were in sight, and the day was abnormally hot, so I sat down and fell asleep in the sun. When I awoke some time later, I found that a ewe with a young lamb had bedded less than one hundred feet (30 meters) away. The two seemed undisturbed when I got up and walked nearby, taking pictures of them. Few wild big game animals ever become so trusting.

Several days later, a cold rain caught me well up on the same Primrose slope. I sat huddled under a poncho, trying to keep myself and my equipment dry until the squall passed. This time a band of fine Dall rams came feeding in my direction. Although they could easily have detoured well around me, all kept coming directly toward the red-plastic-covered, shivering object

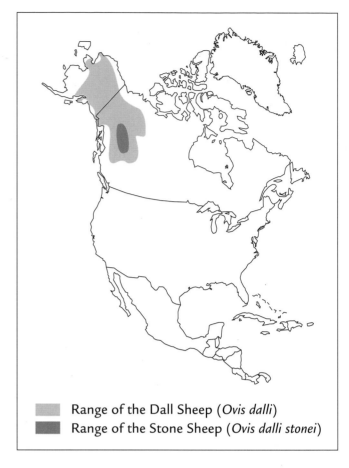

Range of the Dall Sheep (*Ovis dalli*)
Range of the Stone Sheep (*Ovis dalli stonei*)

*Adult front hoof length: Approximately 3 inches (75 mm) Distance between tracks when walking: Approximately 15 inches (375 mm)*

**Track of the Dall Sheep (*Ovis dalli*) and Stone Sheep (*Ovis dalli stonei*)**

in their path. They all calmly moved nearer and then passed on with hardly a glance to the side. One, I estimate, walked within eighteen feet (5 meters) of my soggy boots.

*Facing page, top:* Short summers and bitter winters are the rule in Dall sheep range, such as these mountains in Denali National Park, Alaska. *Facing page, bottom:* Most Dall rams spend summers in small bachelor groups as they are here on Primrose Mountain in Denali National Park. Friends become rivals when the annual rut begins.

## Stone and Fannin Sheep

A granite-colored subspecies of the white sheep, the Stone, *Ovis dalli stonei*, lives in the Cassiar and adjacent mountain ranges of British Columbia. Except for body color, the two are indistinguishable. In fact, the pale gray race of southern Yukon, where ranges of *O.d. dalli* and *O.d. stonei* overlap, was once known as the Fannin sheep. Today, the Fannin is recognized as only an intergradation of the Dall and Stone.

Both Dalls and Stones grow thinner and, on the average, more widespread horns than bighorns. Some biologists classify them as the thin-horned sheep. Older Dall rams usually have long, outward-curling horns. Ewes and the youngest rams have short, slender, slightly smaller horns. How fast and how massive sheep horns grow depends on a combination of heredity, general health, nutrition, and perhaps other factors not yet understood.

In the world of trophy hunters and hunting, the one head that is considered the all-time greatest of all North American trophies is a Stone ram. Both of the horns measured more than fifty inches (125 cm) long. This remarkable sheep was taken by L. S. Chadwick above the Muskwa River in British Columbia in 1936.

*Above: Dall lambs are easily able to follow their mothers soon after birth. Any one that does not soon falls prey to the wolves, wolverines, or grizzly bears sharing their world. Left: A band of Dall ewes and lambs rest in July sunshine, some of the animals always alert while the others doze.*

*The gray, or Stone, sheep is a closely related subspecies of the white Dall and has a similar lifestyle. This old ram carries heavy, curling horns typical of its kind.*

*Stone sheep range is confined largely to inland mountains of British Columbia. This one was spotted along the Alaska Highway near Muncho Lake.*

It is now part of the Boone and Crockett Club's national collection.

My own first glimpse of Stone sheep came in 1953, and it remains an indelible memory. My friend Frank Sayers and I were hunting Stones in the Cassiar Mountains and late one afternoon spotted five rams. All were grazing much lower on a grassy slope than one might expect to find them. While I set up a spotting scope for a better look at the horns, Frank saw something else in his binoculars.

"Wolves," he whispered.

As we watched, a pair of gray wolves slowly worked their way upward behind the sheep. It looked as if the hunters had a good chance at catching the lowest animal, which seemed unaware of any danger. But suddenly the ram was on its feet, alerted perhaps by the sound of a dislodged stone or maybe the wolf scent borne on the wind. In the same split second, all the sheep looked up and began scrambling straight up the mountain face with the wolves just behind them. It was no contest. The sheep easily reached a thin ledge in a cliff area where they stopped and stared down at the wolves, which were unable or unwilling to follow them. It probably does not happen that way all the

*Dall rams spend summer alternately resting and feeding. Daytime bedding sites are invariably made where they can watch for danger approaching from any direction.*

time, but this was a fine example of a wild sheep's survival skills.

Native American hunting guide Charley Abou told me of another revealing incident in that same Cassiar region that occurred early one June a few years earlier. A band of ewes with new lambs was traveling toward their summer range when they came to a mountain stream swollen to a torrent by the warm weather and melting snow. Without hesitation, the females plunged into the stream and with difficulty managed to wade across the powerful current. The lambs followed and despite being washed some distance downstream, three of them made it safely across. At least three others did not and drowned. But all of the sheep, including the mothers who lost their lambs, continued their upward trek without a backward look. It was the survival of the fittest and the strongest.

# PRONGHORN ANTELOPE

## *The Swiftest North American Mammal*

One of my first meetings with pronghorns came unexpectedly on a fragrant, clear, cool morning in central Wyoming. A lone coyote was mousing its way across a sagebrush flat, headed toward a den full of pups some distance away. Suddenly a female pronghorn exploded out of the sage close to the coyote and directly in its path. The startled coyote gave chase, but it was no contest. The fastest North American mammal on four feet easily outran the wild dog, which soon gave up and disappeared over a rise.

As I sat drinking coffee in my parked pickup an hour or so later, the pronghorn returned to the same spot from where she had flushed. As I watched through a spotting scope, a fawn stood up on shaky legs and began to nurse. I realized then that not only did the mother escape the wiliest of wild hunters, she also had saved her fawn. Before too long that fawn also would be able to outdistance a hungry coyote.

The pronghorn, or American antelope, *Antilocapra americana*, is a graceful, lithe, and beautifully designed creature that survives on wide open plains and badlands. The doe that outfoxed the coyote weighed about 80 to 85 pounds (36–38 kg) and stood about three feet (1 meter) at the shoulder. Fully grown bucks weigh 100 to 110 pounds (45–50 kg), although one exceptional Montana buck weighed 160 pounds (72 kg).

The pronghorn is unique in still another important way. It is strictly a North American species without counterpart or close relations anywhere else on earth. In fact, "antelope" is really a misnomer, because the pronghorn is not a true antelope.

*Across open ground, the pronghorn antelope is the fastest mammal on four feet in North America. It is the breeding season here, and the buck at left is attending several females.*

## Back From the Brink of Extinction

We came perilously close to losing this swift, unique, tan-and-white native altogether less than a century ago. The first traders, trappers, and travelers who ventured across the North American Great Plains found pronghorns much less wary than they are today. There were millions of pronghorns then, sharing the land with millions of bison and other game. But frontiersmen and -women shot them first by the wagonload and soon by the trainload. Whole carcasses sold for two bits—25 cents—apiece in cities along the rail lines. Others were shot and left to rot as barbed-wire fences crisscrossed the West and cattle were moved in.

In 1922, naturalist Ernest Thompson Seton estimated that as many as forty million pronghorns had roamed the West before 1800. That figure may be on the high side, but the diaries of explorer John Fremont and many others agree that they were astonishingly abundant. One pioneer wrote they were so numerous that "the foothills in the distance seemed to be moving."

The year I was born, 1919, it seemed that antelope would no longer run across the wide open spaces. In 1921, the first-ever census of the species revealed that only about 22,000 pronghorn survived in sixteen states. By 1925, the number of pronghorns was down to about 10,000 on the entire North American continent. Fortunately, and none too soon, our national conscience at last nagged our politicians to take some action.

A number of United States antelope refuges were established in Nevada and Oregon, and hunting of antelope was stopped everywhere in the country. The animals responded well to the protection. Today, the future of this unique national wildlife treasure is relatively secure. The 1995 population is about 500,000, making them the second most abundant large mammal in the United States, after deer. The original range included most plains habitat from the Mississippi River to California, northern Mexico to Alberta. Today the species's range is greatly reduced; the largest number now exist in Wyoming, with Montana ranking second.

Because all antelope live in wide-open country, it is comparatively easy to count them, especially with the use of light aircraft. What's more, they are more easily captured than other, larger game, and can be released into under-stocked habitat. Therefore, wildlife biologists are better able to study and manage this species than most other large animals.

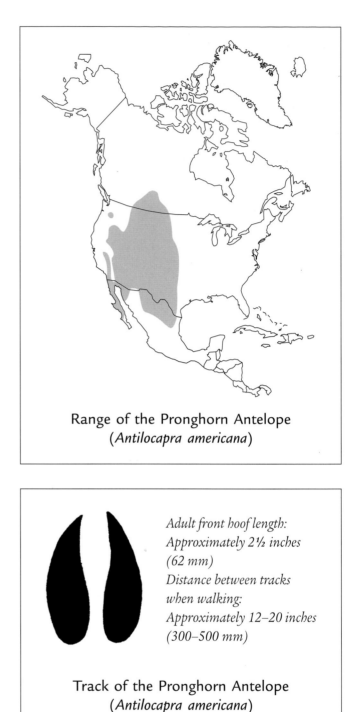

**Range of the Pronghorn Antelope**
(*Antilocapra americana*)

*Adult front hoof length: Approximately 2½ inches (62 mm)*
*Distance between tracks when walking: Approximately 12–20 inches (300–500 mm)*

**Track of the Pronghorn Antelope**
(*Antilocapra americana*)

## The Pronged Horns

The short, pronglike branches midway up the front of the antelope's black horns are what give this species its name. These horns are unique on this continent because the outer black sheath is annually shed from the permanent horn bone beneath. After the shedding in late fall, new, larger sheaths begin to form and after about four or five months they are fully grown and then hardened by summer. Some females also have horns,

*Like all open-country species, this male antelope has the excellent vision necessary to survive on the vast Great Plains of North America.*

but these are never longer than their ears. The horns of a mature buck normally reach twelve inches (30 cm) measured along the front curve, but some top trophies have measured over eighteen inches (45 cm). The maximum longevity of a pronghorn is nine or ten years, but only a few live to be even half that old.

Besides their longer horn length, males are also distinguishable from females by the dark brown to black face mask and the dark cheek patches on each side. Whenever irritated, approached by a rival buck, or when posturing to does, the long hairs on a buck's neck stand erect.

The pronghorn's most distinctive physical characteristic is its ability to "flash," or flare its white rump hair when it is frightened or feels threatened. The instant the antelope senses danger, even if the perceived threat is a long way off, those long white rump hairs flare into a rosette shape that is easily seen from a distance. This serves as a silent warning signal to all other pronghorns in a herd or within view. More than once I

have spotted pronghorns from far away only when one white rump flashed—until then I didn't see them. At other times, curiously, I have watched an obviously frightened herd run away without flashing at all.

When antelope race over the plains, it's a pleasure to watch. Sometimes they do this for no other apparent reason than to exercise or practice their escape routine. Almost goatlike in appearance when standing still or eating, they are born to run—and that includes dashing over rough and uneven terrain. They have a marvelous ability to maneuver or change direction while moving at high speed and to avoid deep mud and quicksand, sharp outcroppings, and dense, brittle brush. Although their thin legs seem fragile, the bones are certainly tough enough to support the animal as it bounds over any topography. Consider the following remarkable experiment.

In a test to determine the maximum load weight an antelope leg bone can bear without breaking, biologist Arthur Einersen was startled by his results. An

antelope foreleg bone withstood over 45,000 pounds per square inch (3,100 kg per 1 cm$^2$). By comparison, the foreleg bone of a domestic cow, which is seven times heavier than that of an antelope, was crushed at much less pressure.

Exactly how fast can a healthy antelope run on its spindly but durable legs? All seem able to move for miles at about twenty miles per hour (32 km/h) without any signs of fatigue. Technicians who have live-captured and relocated many animals assure me that pronghorn can maintain a fast cruising speed of thirty-five miles per hour (56 km/h) over several miles. Even a bedded antelope can spring up suddenly and hit the ground running at this speed. Unlike the bounding of a deer, an antelope's gait begins as a trot: left front, right hind, and so on, quickly striding farther and farther out until the animal is a tan blur. Exactly how fast

*Above: Pronghorns never seem to truly relax. This buck is watching a rival male that is approaching too close to its territory. It later drove the rival away. Left: In winter, antelope often band together in large herds such as this in northern Yellowstone National Park. Not all will survive the extremely cold weather.*

*Coyotes live and thrive in antelope country throughout North America. They take a toll of fawns and old animals weakened by winter, but seldom are a major factor in overall antelope populations.*

it runs depends on how frightened the animal is and how swift the pursuer.

Entire bands have been clocked at fifty to fifty-five miles per hour (80-88 km/h), and that might be the average maximum. Some reliable observers, however, have clocked individual pronghorns at close to sixty miles per hour (96 km/h) and it is possible that a few could be capable of seventy miles per hour (112 km/h) for a short dash.

## Pronghorn Behavior

Fortunately there are antelope herds not far from our home in Montana confiding enough to watch us from a discreet distance rather than run away. A few now pay little attention to us at all. When they are this trusting, I always focus on their large dark eyes, which are as big as those of a saddle horse several times its size. A good many biologists, hunting guides, and this photographer believe that the antelope's phenomenal eyesight is by far the best of any native big game animal. With its eyes set far back on each side of the head, an antelope is able to scan from horizon to horizon without turning its head. There is almost no blind spot from which a predator, human hunter, or rival can approach undetected.

Vision, like the ability to run, is all important in the annual early fall gathering of harems by the strongest males. Sometimes a good bit of sparring and fighting takes place, but it seems less violent to me than the combat between antlered or other horned animals. Harems may consist of only two or three does, or as many as the fifteen we once counted in northern Yellowstone Park.

Fawns are born in early summer and almost immediately one of the shortest infancies among all mammals begins. Within about three days of its birth, any healthy fawn can easily outrun the fastest human.

The nervous nature of pronghorns is reflected in their feeding habits. The animals walk along daintily, taking nips here and there, sometimes even running to a different spot to start again. They do not bite nor pull and uproot edible plants as do other big game

*A young antelope buck pauses in early morning sunshine to scan the horizon for coyotes or human hunters. It is instinctive behavior.*

animals; they simply nibble. Their stomachs are almost always full, indicating that pronghorns eat frequently around the clock rather than during a definite prolonged morning and/or evening period. Sage is one of the most important items in the pronghorn diet, and the eradication of sagebrush to improve cattle grazing in many states has greatly limited antelope populations. Antelope will also browse on such flora as rabbitbrush, saltbrush, bitterbrush, and even juniper, chicory, dandelion, lupine, mullein, and thistle. Compared to the bulk they consume, the dark, hard pellets they leave behind seem to indicate total utilization of the their food.

Despite the antelope's phenomenal vision, speed, and acceleration, they have not adapted to fences and are reluctant to jump them. Fences with crawl space between the lowest wire and the ground do allow antelope to pass. Woven wire fences strung to contain domestic sheep and goats are a serious obstacle along traditional migration routes that antelope use to escape deep snows and find winter survival food. In fact, severe winters in the West can and do take a considerable toll on pronghorn populations. So can the high-speed traffic on a western highway that is laid in a straight line across open country. A single large trailer truck barreling down an interstate in Wyoming can accidentally kill most of a herd that is trapped by walls of plowed snow along the right of way. The higher the legal speed limit, the greater the winter kill of pronghorns.

Long ago, Native American hunters used another antelope trait, its curiosity, as a tool in hunting the pronghorns. A small white goose or eagle feather tied to a sage bush, blowing in the wind, would tempt antelope into coming ever closer for a better look, and into bow and arrow range. The trick still works today. On a number of occasions Peggy and I have been able to bring pronghorns into telephoto lens range by substituting a white handkerchief or tissue for the feather. It doesn't always work, but it has resulted in many good photographs of an interesting big game animal that is found nowhere else on earth.

# MOUNTAIN GOAT

## *The Goat on Top of the World*

A mountain goat in Glacier National Park performed the most athletic feat I have ever witnessed. The animal was standing at the base of an absolutely vertical cliff along the trail to Granite Chalet when a party of noisy hikers came along. They probably were concerned about meeting grizzly bears and so were sounding off and ringing bells as park officials advise. But the goat was frightened and had nowhere to go but up into a narrow canyon that split the cliff.

Without hesitation the goat climbed the canyon wall, bounding to the side, left to right, from ledge to narrow foothold, ricocheting its way to the top without a misstep. Only a bird could have done it any better. From the crest of the cliff the goat paused and looked back down on the hikers who suddenly were silent in awe.

My vote for the most sure-footed large mammal in North America, maybe in the world, goes to this animal, *Oreamnos americanus*, that goat biologist and author Douglas Chadwick described as a "beast the color of winter." No big game animal on this continent spends so much of its life in such high and difficult terrain.

For a long time observers even disagreed on what, exactly, the mountain goat was. Explorer Alexander Mackenzie concluded it was some kind of white buffalo, while Meriwether Lewis and William Clark's crew believed it was a sheep or bear. When coastal Indians brought him goat skins in 1778, Captain James Cook wrote that "there is here a white bear." In fact, the mountain goat is an alpine antelope, and its closest relation is the chamois of Europe.

But by any name, goat or antelope, this animal does not on first sight appear to be athletic. It is as thickset and hump-shouldered as a buffalo and whiskered with a shaggy white coat and short, black, spike horns. Not the least important for its steeplejack lifestyle are the non-skid, suction cup hooves of material similar to tough truck tire rubber. With this equipment, the animal sometimes seems to climb dizzying slopes just for exercise.

*Mountain dwellers of northwestern United States, western Canada, and southeastern Alaska, the all-white mountain goats have no really close relatives anywhere on earth.*

Mountain goats seem to bring out the best phrases of natural history writers. Owen Wister noted that "they choose places to lie down where falling off is the easiest thing to do." An old Alaskan gold miner in the 1890s swore that goats grinned at him when he lost his footing on a mountainside, fell, and broke his arm. More than once after long tense climbs to photograph goats, I have reached a sudden dead end and, in near panic, wondered how I would ever get back down again. I don't think even the least agile mountain goat ever feels this stab of anxiety.

Despite its agility, a mountain goat at first seems clumsy or ponderous. For most of the year, the animals live at the highest elevations where enough nutritious alpine vegetation exists to sustain them. During summer, the males, or billies, usually separate into small groups, but not always; often a male can be found among, if not leading, a larger herd of females and young. The social structure of this species seems to vary a great deal in different parts of their range in the northwestern United States, western Canada, and southeastern Alaska.

## Goats Through the Seasons

The rutting season in late fall everywhere is an exciting time, but is not easily or often observed. Males that were bachelor friends throughout the summer suddenly are rivals. They posture stiff legged, spar, and slash at low brush with spiked horns. Compared to the lunging and crashing horns of wild sheep, this dueling of goats seems almost comical. But those pointed black horns can be deadly and casualties surely must happen. The winners do most if not all of the breeding as the females, or nannies, come into heat.

About six months after the last female is bred, kids weighing seven or eight pounds (3–3½ kg) are dropped on remote mountainsides. Twin kids are not uncommon. Few wild babies are born in such precarious situations and with such a lofty view of the world below. Most newborns are able to stand firmly within ten minutes and some are already jumping around, testing their legs, when only a half hour old. They are weaned in about one month.

Toward the end of May, when the Going-to-the-Sun Highway across Glacier National Park is completely cleared of snow and open to travel, Peggy and I often drive to Logan Pass and from there hike out to find the goat families that spend summers here. It is always an exciting time.

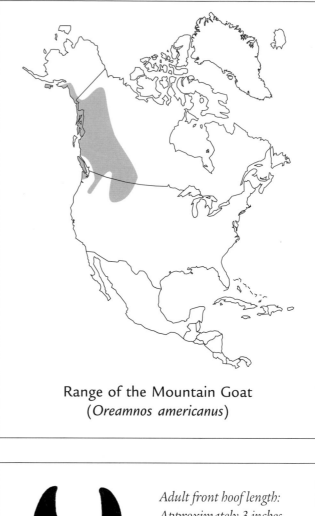

Range of the Mountain Goat
(*Oreamnos americanus*)

*Adult front hoof length: Approximately 3 inches (75 mm)*
*Distance between tracks when walking: Approximately 15 inches (375 mm)*

Track of the Mountain Goat
(*Oreamnos americanus*)

Although protective at times, goat mothers do not always closely supervise their young. While they feed on the new green grasses and forbs that grow where the snow has just melted, the young spend hours gamboling, jumping, and butting one another across snowfields, over loose rock slides, and on top of the steepest ridges. Some of this play is rough and confrontational; social rank or status among the kids seems to be determined in this way early on. Eventually the gangs get tired and take a recess to find their mothers and nurse.

*Above:* A billy stands on the edge of eternity in Olympic National Park, Washington, looking down on mountain mists and the Pacific Ocean far below. Goats are not native here, and many are being removed to prevent damage to the mountain environment. *Left:* Goats seek isolation in places such as British Columbia's Bugaboo Mountains even though the vegetation for browsing is thin and living is hard.

If the day is sunny and warm they might also take a nap with their mother, usually on a narrow ledge where no prowling grizzly bear can sneak up on them. I have watched mothers trying to sleep while their young climb all over them.

Goats probably do not have many natural enemies. Golden eagles, bears, or wolverines may capture the occasional kid that wanders too far from its mother. Cougars may be the most successful wild goat hunters. But avalanches are an important cause of death at all seasons. One explanation offered for this is that a goat's hearing, unlike its eyesight, is poor, and the rumble of an oncoming large rock slide can engulf an entire herd before they hear it coming and can escape.

One morning following heavy spring rains, British Columbia fishing guide Thad Munn had a clear view of what may be a fairly typical goat tragedy. While walking beside a salmon stream, Munn could see a herd of the white animals scattered widely over the face of a

**Both photos:** *It is early summer, and a mother goat watches over the most agile of young mammals. Kids spend days playing leap frog, gamboling, and butting heads, all in preparation for a rugged life.*

41

*Above:* Searching for goats takes a photographer or hunter into the continent's most awesome scenery, as here around Marmolata Pinnacle in British Columbia. **Right:** From a nearly vertical cliff in Glacier National Park, Montana, a solitary goat looks down on hikers using a busy trail far below near Logan Pass.

cliff. Then the center of the cliff began to fall away, the saturated earth with its burden of rock and scrub vegetation moving downward, at first in slow motion, then gaining speed, and finally thundering to the valley below. The goats standing in the middle of the herd simply vanished. The survivors at the edges calmly walked away in opposite directions.

While studying goats and winter mortality for his book, *A Beast the Color of Winter*, Montana biologist Doug Chadwick was cross-country skiing in Glacier Park on a glittering bright day in April. When he spotted a familiar nanny ahead, he paused to scrape off the wet snow that had balled up on his skis. That pause probably saved his life—but not the goat's, as the mountainside just ahead gave way and became a nightmare of falling rocks and ice.

Chadwick estimates that mountain snow and avalanches cause 65 percent of all goat deaths. Much of the best goat country, especially along the Pacific coast, also are areas of high precipitation. At times a single storm can drop three or four feet (90-120 cm) of wet snow overnight, which can cause avalanches. Or the snowfall can trap goats in areas where fat reserves alone keep them alive until they can make their way to more open terrain. Only half of all kids born in spring survive to reach one year of age.

Goats are not immune to intense cold, but they can stand far more of it for longer than a human can comprehend. The dense, shaggy coat protects the animal from both the subfreezing temperatures and wind chills of the wildest winter storms. A healthy goat's coat consists of a fleecy undercoat that is four inches (10 cm) or so thick and compares with the finest cashmere or merino wool. On top of the fleece is an outer coat of long white hair that sheds moisture. It is extraordinary how such warm protection is manufactured from the seemingly sparse diet of small alpine plants, mosses, and scrub.

## Dagger Horns

Unlike other native big game species, goats live a sort of constantly adversarial lifestyle. Males especially seem born to butt one another, especially unfamiliar billies. But any goat that happens to be in the way, including a kid, is likely to feel the horns of another. Once when studying a band of eight goats in western Montana's Swan Mountains, Chadwick saw two dozen fights break out in one hour, some in precipitous places. A number of the encounters ended with visible puncture wounds from the sharp horns, but none of the combatants were pushed over the edge.

Both sexes have horns, but it is usually possible to tell them apart. Male horns are larger, especially at the base, and curve gradually backward to a maximum length of twelve inches (30 cm). The distance between the horns of females is greater than that of the males, and the nannies' horns themselves are thinner and curve more sharply to the rear.

The all-white goats usually are seen against a darker background, and this makes the animals appear larger than they are. Still, an animal that reaches 200 to 250 pounds (90-110 kg) or even more, even without the dagger horns, is a formidable creature to meet on a narrow mountain trail wide enough for only one. During photography in Glacier, Olympic, and Kluane National Parks, we have always managed to avoid such a meeting.

There is a mineral lick along the highway near Essex, Montana, that is often visited by the goats of southern Glacier Park. One afternoon in March 1992, photographers Jim Mepham and Steve Torna were watching a herd of about thirty approach the lick, and they began to shoot them with telephoto lenses. Suddenly the goats bolted in all directions. Mepham soon saw the reason for the panic: A mountain lion was on the back of one of the goats. Eventually the lion brought the goat down. Crouched over its kill, the cat looked up directly toward the photographers, snarled, and walked away. Unsure about its future intentions, the two men also backed away.

The lion had its eyes on another nanny that had climbed onto a rock outcrop. While camera shutters clicked, the tawny cat pounced on the second goat and both went rolling down a steep slope. At the bottom, the cat was on top of its dying prey. Flushed with adrenaline and realizing they had seen the rarest of wild encounters, the two men retreated to their car. Just to see a mountain lion in the wild is a rare event and they are almost never photographed in the wild, so photographing a double kill is a once-in-a-billion opportunity. The cat remained in the area for four days until it had eaten all of the goat meat. But perhaps the most remarkable thing about the Glacier Park kills was that animals born to butt one another, where physical confrontation is a part of daily life in the herd, did not seem to fight back at all. "The goats didn't squeal," according to Torna, "they didn't struggle, and they didn't kick. All at once it was all over."

# BUFFALO

## *Monarch of the Great Plains*

In 1521, during his conquest of Central America, Spanish conquistador Hernán Cortés visited the menagerie of Aztec ruler Montezuma. One beast he saw there, according to a seventeenth-century chronicler of the expedition, was "the Mexican Bull, a wonderful composition of divers Animals. It has crooked shoulders, with a Bunch on its Back like a Camel; its Flanks dry, its Tail large, and its Neck cover'd with Hair like a Lion." That creature was *Bison bison*, the American bison, or buffalo, and almost certainly Cortés was the first European to see the species. But like the waves of Europeans who would follow him to the New World, his interest was not in wildlife, but in wealth—mainly in gold.

The bison itself was an immigrant. It reached North America from Eurasia more than a million years ago via a land bridge that once connected present-day Siberia with Alaska. The alien herds gradually moved southward, eventually colonizing most of the continent, especially the great central and western plains. In time, bison ranged from northern Mexico far northward into Canada and from Oregon almost to the Atlantic Coast. In the 1830s, Virginia settler William Byrd wrote: "This is a fine place for Cattle and Hoggs and fortunately there is a large Creature of the Beef kind, but much larger, called a Buffalo, which may be bred up tame and is good both for food and labour."

When landholder Byrd was writing that letter, the number of bison roaming wild just to the west was at least ten million, according to the *lowest* latter day estimate, and possibly as high as sixty million, as some historians believe. Early travelers in the American West wrote of riding across landscapes on which almost nothing else was visible but the dark bodies of bison and plumes of dust. Such scenes as this were common until about 1870. Barely ten years later virtually all of the buffalo were gone.

*A powerful, mature bull bison is a survivor of the great herds that once roamed from horizon to horizon across the North American plains.*

The story of the buffalo's slaughter is well known. The bison were killed for several reasons: meat for Americans expanding westward, hides for the market, to clear the land for domestic cattle, to demoralize the Indians who depended on them for survival and, far too often, just for the hell of it. To many, the animals seemed as inexhaustible and as useless as locusts—and potentially dangerous besides.

Never in history has there been such a slaughter of wildlife at the hands of humans. In 1869, Civil War hero General Phil Sheridan declared that "every buffalo dead is an Indian gone." Almost always it is the loss or degradation of habitat that pushes wild animals toward or into extinction. But in this case the near obliteration was accomplished by shooting alone.

## "Strong Medicine"

The powerful, shaggy animal we almost lost, the one on which the Cheyenne, Sioux, Kiowas, Blackfoot, Comanches, and all other plains tribes valued and depended upon, stood more than five feet (150 cm) at the shoulder and weighed from 1,000 to 2,000 pounds (450-900 kg) when fully grown. The bulls were much larger than the cows. Buffaloes simply were "strong medicine," and impressive no matter how they were viewed.

Native Americans ate buffalo meat fresh and raw,

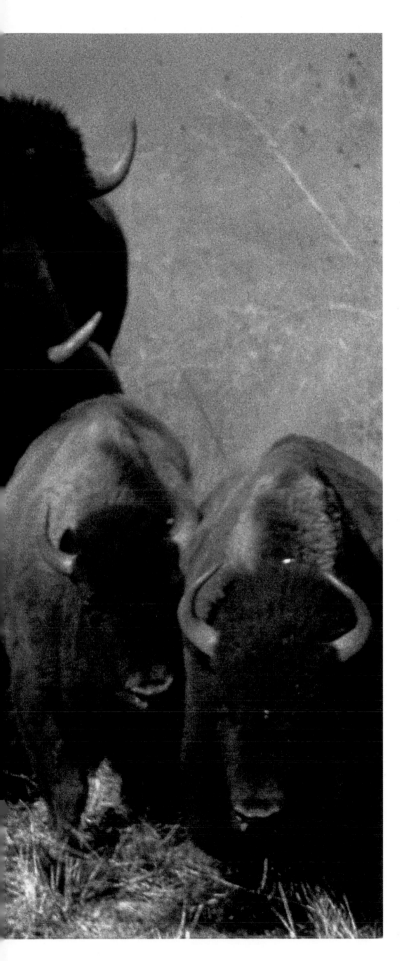

*Above:* During dry summers, a herd of bison on the move can raise dust clouds that obscure the sun. Sometimes the noise of such a thundering herd is audible from far away. *Left:* Spooked by thunderstorms and grassfire, a herd of buffaloes stampedes over rolling grasslands in late summer at the National Bison Range, Montana.

often consumed right where the animal was killed. Or they smoked or sun-dried the meat, or pounded it and mixed it with wild berries and fat to make pemmican. They tanned the hides and sewed them with buffalo sinew into dresses and shirts, leggings and moccasins, eventually into saddles and tacking. The winter "robes" of buffaloes kept Native Americans warm during the most bitter winters as they slept in teepees of scraped buffalo hides. The tough, thickest hide from a male bison's neck was made into warriors' shields that deflected arrows and even some lead bullets. Lighter rawhide went into cooking pots, crude canteens and containers, ropes, and arrow quivers. Glue and waterproofing came from boiling hooves. Horns were used as ladles and rib bones as sled runners. Bowstrings were made of bison sinew. Bison tails and hair decorated horses and headdresses. Tails were also used as whips or fly swatters.

Life was a desperate struggle for both people and beasts on the vast North American plains. Blizzards, droughts, wind-driven prairie fires, rivers choked with ice in winter or swollen with spring rains—all took a great toll of buffaloes each year. But bison were prolific and abundant enough to withstand large losses and sustain the Indians as well. Until the winning of the West began, that is.

Toward the end of the nineteenth century, only a few small and scattered wild buffalo populations remained in remote areas, most notably in Yellowstone National Park and Wood Buffalo National Park, north of Great Slave Lake in northern Alberta. The latter was the final stronghold of the debated subspecies, wood bison, *Bison bison athabasca*, a slightly larger buffalo. A good bit of what we know today about buffaloes living in the wild as they had for centuries comes from watching the herds in Yellowstone, at the National Bison Range in Moiese, Montana, at Custer State Park, South Dakota, and at the Wichita Mountains National Wildlife Refuge in Oklahoma.

## Buffaloes Through the Season

Every August, Peggy and I strive to be in Yellowstone's Hayden Valley to witness the annual rutting season. Despite the fact that as many tourists as bison cause

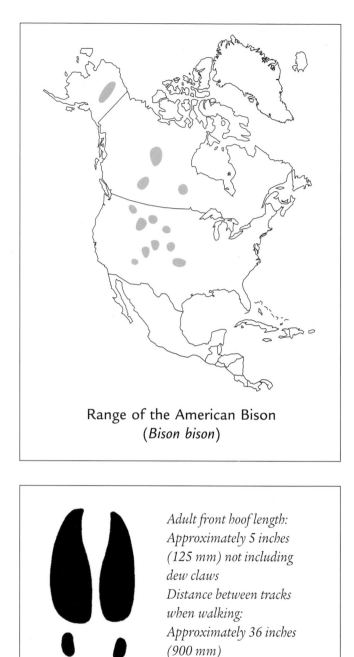

Range of the American Bison
(*Bison bison*)

*Adult front hoof length:*
*Approximately 5 inches*
*(125 mm) not including*
*dew claws*
*Distance between tracks*
*when walking:*
*Approximately 36 inches*
*(900 mm)*

Track of the American Bison (*Bison bison*)

traffic jams along the road that parallels the Yellowstone River here, it is always exciting. Bachelor bulls that have spent the previous winter and summer apart from the other bison now join the large cow and calf herds to challenge the herd bulls. Thus, a lot of chasing,

*Facing page, top: Winter is the hunger moon, a time when starvation looms everywhere in bison range. This herd is wintering along the Firehole River in Yellowstone National Park. Facing page, bottom: Mothers are stubborn defenders of bison calves. The calves follow their mothers closely during their first summer.*

*In sanctuaries such as Yellowstone National Park, buffaloes still roam far and wide as they have for centuries. They will even swim large rivers to find better grazing.*

maneuvering, and violent head-to-head butting takes place in countless tournaments in an arena that may cover a hundred acres (40 hectares) or more. Dust swirls. Herds cross and recross the Yellowstone River as the center of rutting action shifts.

As the cows come into estrus, they are constantly accompanied by bulls that shield them from all other suitors. A deep-throated sound, almost like a continuous moan, hangs in the air as the bulls voice their excitement. Cow bison that are ready to mate are mounted and impregnated by the bulls that have dominated the others and survived the fighting. Altogether the buffalo rut is more like a melee or mob scene when compared to the more ritualized elk rut that will take place nearby a few weeks later.

After the rut ends, the herds have a peaceful respite for about two months to graze and rebuild body fat before early winter arrives with its heavy snows. By using their powerful shoulders and neck muscles, the bison bulldoze deep snow with their heads, uncovering whatever grass remains beneath the snow. Winter

always takes a grim toll on the weaker animals; each year a percentage of them will slowly starve and not survive. This is a boon to the hungry coyotes, foxes, eagles, magpies, and ravens that quickly find any fallen buffalo. Now that wolves have been reintroduced to Yellowstone, they also are preying upon winter-weakened animals.

Spring is welcomed by the bison for the growth of new food, and soon, nine months after the rut, rusty-red calves are born in May or June. The calves somewhat resemble domestic calves except for their shorter necks. But soon they are a lot more agile and mobile than any young Herefords or shorthorns. By September, the calves' coats are dark brown, covering the beginnings of their buffalo humps. Most also have short spike horns that will eventually grow much heavier and longer, up to nineteen or twenty inches (47–50 cm) on males. The bulls reach their prime at between six and ten years old. A few individuals in captivity have been known to live thirty years, but it's doubtful if any free roaming bison can survive that many brutal winters,

*Daybreak in the Hayden Valley, Yellowstone. A bachelor bull wanders along Trout Creek, seeking to join up with a resident herd.*

especially where predators also live.

Bison seem to revel in summer. The green grass will never be more lush or more nutritious. All buffaloes shed their heavy winter coats and for a brief time have a seedy look. Discarded hair is blown away by the wind and snagged by sagebrush as the animals brush past. Some birds use it to line their nests. To speed the shedding and maybe also because it feels good, the bison scratch against trees (causing heavy damage in places), roll in dusty wallows, and plaster themselves with mud, probably also as relief from insects. As the herds graze, cowbirds, blackbirds, and starlings follow, occasionally catching a free ride on a buffalo's back in exchange for spearing ticks. On hot days the bison rest for many hours and become more active at night.

## Looking to a Healthy Future

Although there is no chance whatever that bison would ever roam the North American plains as they did long ago, the species is fairly secure. Buffalo ranching has become a profitable business because the animals are not as destructive to their range as an equal number of domestic cattle, and the bison's tasty meat has less fat.

In addition to Yellowstone and Canada's Wood Buffalo National Park, there are several other places where bison herds can be seen. The National Bison Range in Montana is the best site of all with an eighteen-mile (29-km) one-way road through typical open bison range shared with antelope, elk, bighorn sheep, and deer. Equally good is Custer State Park with its large, healthy herd in South Dakota's Black Hills, along with nearby Wind Cave National Park and Badlands National Park. Other ranges include Sully's Hill Game Refuge and Theodore Roosevelt National Park, both in North Dakota; Grand Teton National Park and Thermopolis State Park, Wyoming; and Waterton and Elk Island National Parks in Alberta, Canada. The bison herds that we see today look much as they must have appeared to the Native Americans of the plains and the first white people to encounter the great beasts. We are fortunate to have this "virtual reality" today.

# MUSKOXEN

## *Mammoth Oxen of the Arctic*

One of the least known of North American big game species is one that lives only in the most remote places, far from human development. Superficially resembling buffaloes, muskoxen, *Ovibos moschatus*, are circumpolar and native to both Alaska and the Canadian Arctic, where as many as ten thousand roam over the Thelon Game Sanctuary and on Banks and Ellesmere Islands, all in the Northwest Territory.

The last herd of eighteen Alaskan muskoxen were killed by trappers near Chandalar Lake during the 1890s. But thirty-four animals were transported from Greenland in 1936 to Nunivak Island and this herd has prospered. From this beginning, about one thousand live on Nunivak today. From here surplus animals have also been reintroduced onto Nelson Island, Seward Peninsula, the Cape Lisbourne–Cape Thompson area, and Arctic National Wildlife Refuge of northern Alaska.

The origin of the name muskox is a mystery, because the species has no musk. Some early Arctic explorers did report musk glands in the skin, under the eyes, in the feet, and even claimed that the meat tasted strongly of musk. This myth has been repeated by adventure writers ever since. Eskimos who guided us during April photo expeditions to Nunivak in 1967 and 1989 assured us that the meat was as "sweet" as any beef shipped to the island from the mainland.

Muskoxen typically stand three and a half feet (105 cm) at the shoulder and weigh from 400 to 800 pounds (180–360 kg), males being larger than females. All have horns that curve downward and then outward and are shaped like handlebar moustaches; the horns may measure thirty inches (75 cm) long on the oldest bulls, ending in sharp points. But what sets muskoxen apart from any other species in the animal kingdom is its long hair coat, which is also its most striking feature.

*A big game animal that nobody really knows, the muskoxen today lives only in the loneliest regions of Arctic Canada and on a few Alaskan islands. This one is a large herd bull.*

Guard hairs as long as two feet (60 cm)—the longest of any continental species—hang down almost to the ground in winter. The hairs also form beards and manes on males that accentuate the humps on their shoulders. One cold morning, Peggy and I were photographing a female on Nunivak Island and for a long while, until the ox moved, we did not see the newborn calf that stood nursing, completely hidden beneath the mother's ground-sweeping guard hairs.

Underneath the dark, outer hair is a much finer, lighter-colored underhair called qiviut (pronounced *kivi-oot*). During summer, the animals have a distinctly ragged look as the old qiviut is shed and the new underhair replaces it. Wherever muskoxen live, long streamers of qiviut catch on vegetation and blow in the Arctic wind. Some birds use it to insulate nests, and natives gather it to spin into yarn to make the warm, soft mittens, caps, and scarves.

The combination of long outer hairs and dense, warm qiviut beneath enables muskoxen to withstand gale force winds and -50°F (-45°C) temperatures for long periods. In those same places, summertime temperatures may soar over 80°F (26°C) for several days.

## Muskoxen Through the Seasons

During the brief northern summer, muskoxen are most likely to be found in the more lush vegetation along streams where salmon may be spawning and clouds of mosquitoes whine. They nibble on dwarf birch, willow, and Arctic grasses, especially around coastal cliffs where great colonies of seabirds nest and fertilize the surrounding area. During dark winters when the sun may seldom shine for weeks, muskoxen are again driven to coastal dune areas where incessant winds clear the snow and expose beach rye grass on which they graze. Surprisingly, these hardy animals cannot cope with deep snow.

August is the rutting season. The rutting bulls continually fight and pursue females, trying to herd and keep as many as possible in personal harems. It is a turbulent time, because harem bulls and challengers fight as violently as bighorn rams—maybe even more so. After bluffing, snorting, and shoving preliminaries, two or more of the strongest bulls back apart and

Range of the Muskoxen
(*Ovibos moschatus*) in North America

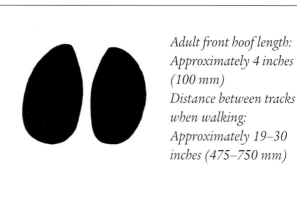

*Adult front hoof length: Approximately 4 inches (100 mm)*
*Distance between tracks when walking: Approximately 19–30 inches (475–750 mm)*

Track of the Muskoxen (*Ovibos moschatus*)

then race toward each other at high speed, smashing the bases of their horns together. This may be repeated as many as twenty times in a single contest, which would seem to cripple both of the battlers. But the only injury suffered seems to be the loss of dignity when

*Facing page, top:* Inuit natives of Canada's Far North once hunted muskoxen with dogs. They hunted from tundra camps such as this one near Bathurst Inlet, Northwest Territories. *Facing page, bottom:* A human's approach causes muskoxen to form the same defensive circle they have used to coexist with wolves and barren ground grizzlies for thousands of years.

the loser skulks away.

Before humans came upon the scene with firearms, muskoxen defended themselves in a unique and effective way. When beset by a pack of wolves, for example, the herd would form into a defensive circle with calves huddled in the middle and all others facing outward toward the attackers. This was an excellent strategy for tens of thousands of years. It later made the animals easy targets for a hunter with sled dogs and a rifle who could shoot the entire stationery herd. Now muskoxen around the world also must deal with hunters on snowmobiles.

Bulls that cannot acquire harems gather into small male herds or live lonely bachelor lives, and these are the individuals that require plenty of room. They are faster on their feet than seems possible for such large beasts, and they are often in a bad humor. That word to the wise muskox hunter or photographer should be sufficient.

*Above: In early summer, muskoxen, such as this large bull, shed the fine undercoat of hair (called* qiviut*); Inuit natives gather the qiviut to make warm garments. New hair replaces the old before another winter begins.* **Left:** *On Nunivak Island's coast, a herd of muskoxen instinctively form a defensive circle to protect themselves from wolves. Adults face outward protecting the young within.*

# WHITETAILED DEER

## *North America's Favorite Deer*

It was a cold December morning for central Texas and a chill wind was howling through the bare oaks. Rancher and old friend Allen Grimland and I had been sitting and shivering in a blind on a grassy knoll since well before daybreak. Between us and a dark oak woods where acorns littered the ground, Allen had filled a feeder with corn and pellets. For several weeks he had been watching and trying to bait a huge whitetail buck into this area, and now I was trying to photograph it. I sat behind my tripod-mounted camera with the 600mm lens poking out through a small opening in the blind.

From time to time does came to our bait and then, with bellies full, drifted away. A ten-point buck also came, but it was not the big one we were hoping to see. By mid-morning, I was thoroughly chilled, cramped, and ready to give up the vigil until dusk. Of course that was when Allen nudged me with an elbow and pointed to my left. I turned slowly and spotted the deer that seemed to be staring directly at us. He was very suspicious.

I have seen and focused on many fine whitetails over the years, but I am convinced that this one had the biggest typical (both sides symmetrical) antlers I have ever witnessed outside of a trophy room. When the animal came into sharp focus in my viewfinder, I counted six points on each side before I squeezed the shutter. The antler beams were heavy and I estimated they spread more than two feet (60 cm) apart. I squeezed off an exposure, another, and suddenly the metallic sound of the camera motor drive seemed to annoy the animal. It looked toward where a doe was feeding on corn. Then as mysteriously as it had arrived on the scene, it vanished. What I felt next was similar to the buck fever I felt when looking at my first set of wild antlers more than a half century ago.

*A large whitetail buck crowned with a tall rack of nontypical antlers.*

Over hot coffee later, Allen and I talked about whitetails. We agreed that there is no big game species in North America, or maybe anywhere, to match a buck that has survived enough hunting seasons to reach the trophy size we had just seen. It is easy to understand why this species, *Odocoileus virginianus*, is so popular (and sometimes so unpopular and unwelcome) all across the continent. Whole magazines, books, and countless videos are devoted to whitetail hunting, and every fall hunters spend millions of dollars on their sport. No other species has accumulated such a mystique and such a cult following.

## Whitetail Characteristics

Scientists have divided the species *O. virginianus* into thirty different subspecies. Many of these subspecies are isolated on ocean islands or in small environments in Central America where they have not been studied thoroughly. Study specimens of some are rare and some others in collections may be incorrectly identified.

There is still another problem with separating subspecies. Generally speaking, the largest deer on average with the largest racks today tend to live in central Canada, *O.v. dakotensis*. The smallest, no larger than setter dogs, are the miniature deer of southern Florida's Keys, the Key deer, *O.v. clavium*. But within the United States and Canada, no other creature in our history has been so often planted, transplanted, interbred, stocked, and restocked, from Minnesota to Georgia, from Saskatchewan to Texas, to breed and interbreed. Record keeping of all this is scanty, inaccurate, or missing altogether, so we must think of the whitetail as a single species—one whitetail, *Odocoileus virginianus*, the greatest and most graceful big game animal on our continent.

There are a number of reasons for the whitetail's renown. First, it's an attractive mammal. It's also elusive, and the older and bigger the animal, the more this is true. And whitetails are abundant; there probably are more of them in the world in the late 1990s than at any time since they evolved from small, piglike ancestors millions of years ago.

If you doubt this unlikely ancestry, consider the similarities between deer and swine today. Both animals have split, cloven hooves that leave tracks on the

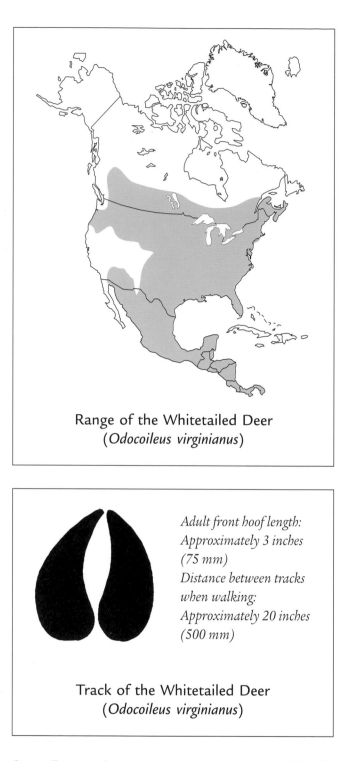

Range of the Whitetailed Deer
(*Odocoileus virginianus*)

*Adult front hoof length: Approximately 3 inches (75 mm)*
*Distance between tracks when walking: Approximately 20 inches (500 mm)*

Track of the Whitetailed Deer
(*Odocoileus virginianus*)

forest floor. In fact, many woodsmen have trouble telling apart the tracks of deer and those of pigs. The animals share a keen sense of smell, excellent eyesight, and astute hearing. Both have elongated skulls, compact bodies, and short, stiff hair. The legs of deer and swine are similar in structure, although the whitetail's are

*During severe winters, whitetails often gather in "yards," or groups, for protection from cold winds and for mutual security. In spite of this tactic, not all will survive.*

longer. Whenever a domestic hog escapes into the wild, it prefers the same kind of habitat as whitetails. Their vocalizations are similar, and both live on highly varied diets. Both are favored prey of large predators.

Although modern whitetails mainly are woodland browsers, they can adapt to twentieth-century agriculture, thriving on anything from corn to alfalfa to soybeans and sweet potatoes, and from orchard fruit to ornamental shrubbery—which wins them few friends in suburbia. We have found healthy deer herds in northern cedar bogs and in southern canebrakes, throughout suburbia, in high western meadows, and on river floodplains everywhere. You see them lurking in farm fence rows and windbreaks. While writing this book, I have been able to watch whitetails out of my office window in Paradise Valley, Montana, almost every day.

In fact, this prolific species is found wild in every American state but Alaska and Hawaii, all across southern and central Canada, southward throughout Mexico and Central America to the Amazon Basin. The farthest-north whitetail appearance on record was a deer killed in an auto collision near Watson Lake on the Yukon–British Columbia border in 1994. Of larger North American mammals, only coyotes and raccoons are able to adapt to—and outwit people in—as many different environments. Whitetails are almost certainly

the most numerous of large mammals living on earth today.

It is impossible to spend much time among these deer and not marvel at their great physical abilities and toughness. Childhood tales and entertainment such as poor Bambi tell us that this is a frail, defenseless creature barely making out in a cruel world. The truth is that they are the toughest survivors, excellent athletes able to cope with just about everything except the loss of environment and the high-speed traffic on superhighways.

A healthy whitetail is swift afoot and a powerful leaper. It is true that pronghorns can cover more miles

per hour in open country, but I have always wondered if any big game animal can match the speed of a really frightened whitetail as it bounds over the deadfalls and rock piles in a dense second-growth forest, seemingly without effort and with single leaps of twenty-five feet (7½ meters) or more. Some whitetails we have encountered escaped this way; others seemed to dissolve into the background.

Most of the time, sudden danger causes instant reaction, sudden running flight. No matter how fast the animal runs, it can abruptly change direction without slowing down, a maneuver that could snap most legs. But this and other acrobatics are routine for the whitetail, because its slim forelegs do not connect directly to the skeleton. Instead, they are separated by a tough, resilient cartilage that acts as a cushion or shock absorber.

*Above:* Antlers of whitetail males grow into many shapes and sizes. This Texas buck sports especially high—rather than wide—antlers. **Left:** Whitetails are inexorably extending their original range westward, as here into the Yellowstone River valley in south central Montana, where they are now numerous.

*A Texas buck instinctively takes advantage of long shadows to remain inconspicuous while bedded on the edge of an oak woods.*

Every healthy whitetail depends on excellent hearing, a phenomenal sense of smell, and good eyesight, even after night falls. The ears are like small satellite dishes, turning in all directions to catch any sounds. Some people believe that the whitetail's vision is flawed in that it may not be able to spot a strange or unfamiliar object, say a hunter or wild predator, until the object moves. Many times, by sitting absolutely motionless, Peggy and I have had deer approach within good photography range only to race away when we slowly raised and aimed a camera.

It is almost impossible to exaggerate how keenly a deer hears. A doe caring for a fawn can tell if the footfall she detects in the distance was made by another deer in the herd or by a human, farm dog, or black bear—she has the vital knowledge of whether the sound comes from friend or foe.

Deer do not always run when danger arrives, and that is a good point to remember when hunting them. More than once we have seen deer, older ones especially, that simply drift out of sight rather than bolt. A buck might also stand motionless, or drop down into a crouch if the cover is thick, until any stalkers have passed. I always wonder how many deer I have passed unseen in the wild as they used this strategy.

One fall morning in South Texas, Peggy and I sat in our van on the edge of a sendero where deer, including at least two heavy bucks, came daily to feed. This morning two dozen wary females—but no males—came to our bait of corn. As we were preparing to leave, Peggy happened to notice the glint of sunlight on smooth antlers. All the while a well-hidden buck had been watching us, motionless, from less than one hundred feet (30 meters) away.

## The Majestic Crown of Antlers

What sets whitetails, as well as mule deer, elk, moose, and caribou, apart from all other living things is that the males of this international family, *Cervidae*, grow and discard antlers every year as long as they live. No

*Even in southeastern forests, whitetails may gather in large herds, especially where they are attracted by artificial feeding, as here in Louisiana.*

other animals do this. Among *Cervidae* females, only caribou also grow antlers, but even at their largest they are much smaller than those of males. Of course there are occasional aberrations; no hunting season ever passes in North America without a few antlered whitetail does being shot by surprised hunters. But this is most uncommon.

Unlike horns, deer antlers are true bone—they are in fact the fastest-growing bone known to science. Antlers are also deciduous. That is, a whitetail buck's antlers grow for about four months in summer while covered with velvet, harden, and then are lost or cast about six months after growth began. They then are replaced with a new set. Normally, a buck's first antlers appear in spring when the deer is one year old. These first antlers are small and modest in size, as early in life most of a deer's nutrition goes into building a strong body rather than into antler formation.

No two sets of deer antlers are exactly the same in size, shape, and weight. But if the animal is healthy and lives on suitable range, each new set of antlers will grow faster and be heavier than that of the previous year until the animal reaches its prime at five and a half or six and a half years of age. The longer the animal lives beyond that (and not many do), the smaller the successive antlers. Antler size is actually only the roughest indication of a deer's age; true age can only be determined by a careful examination of its teeth.

Throughout a buck whitetail's life, the general conformation of its antlers, as well as any other irregularities, will remain pretty much the same. Observant deer hunters who go afield every year in the same area are often able to identify individual deer.

While deer antlers are actually growing, they are covered with a short-haired modified skin called velvet. It grows from skin on the deer's skull, around the pedicles, or antler bases, dries and dies when the antler stops growing, and either falls or is rubbed off by the deer. It always seemed to me that the furry look of the velvet, especially on larger bucks and particularly in

*Many whitetails spend much, if not most, of their lives in dim forests, emerging only after dark. Some large bucks actually become nocturnal.*

*The velvet of summer still covers the antlers of this splendid whitetail buck, which is about six and a half years old and has twenty antler points on its nontypical rack.*

bright sunshine, makes them far more conspicuous in a green summer woods than in fall when the velvet is gone.

Ever since the French naturalist Buffon declared in the 1700s that deer antlers were made of wood because of the bark (velvet) that was shed, evolutionists and biologists have debated and disagreed on the reason for antlers. Self defense might seem a logical reason, but bucks are without their antlers in winter when both sexes seem to need them most to protect them against predators. I once watched a buck beset by a pack of feral dogs defend itself by thrusting with its front hooves rather than using its antlers, as I would have

expected. Does also use their front hooves. Consider too that most whitetails have inward-curved antlers rather than tines that point forward, which would be best for effective combat in spearing another animal.

The probable answer is that all deer have antlers for display: to advertise their size to potential rivals and then for fighting those rivals if the other signs and signals fail to carry the message.

I have watched whitetails clash many times, and most of the fights are brief. We have also seen a few vicious, noisy battles between bucks of similar size, with lunging and twisting that resulted in the loser, or even both combatants, being injured. But no matter whether

*Only a week or so old, this whitetail fawn surveys the green world in northern Minnesota where it will spend the rest of its life. Its mother is feeding nearby.*

it is a brief shoving match or a donnybrook, I sense that the two take some care to lock antlers in a way that avoids slippage and more serious damage around the face. Still, one of the largest wild whitetails I have even seen was blind in one eye and had a badly damaged ear.

## Whitetails Through the Seasons

The rut is certainly an exciting time to watch deer. There are plenty of theories about what actually triggers the rut—weather, biostimulation, sex ratio, and so on—but no matter which is correct, it is a time of greatly increased travel and activity, particularly among males,

which are less wary or more distracted than at any other time of year. It is an especially good time if you go afield to photograph deer, and fortunately the onset of the mating season is fairly predictable because it varies with geographic latitude.

The time of the rutting season probably evolved so that most of the new fawns would miss the end-of-winter storms, the spring flooding, and summer's worst insect hatches. With few exceptions, the rut begins earlier in the north than in the south. Within the band of states from Pennsylvania to Oregon and including Canada, the whitetail rut begins from late October and continues into November. In the narrower band from

Ohio and New Jersey south to Tennessee and the Carolinas, the rut begins a month later. In most of Texas (except eastern Texas, where it takes place earlier as in the Midwestern band), the Southwest and Mexico, rutting takes place in December and January. From central Mexico southward, it is a year-round activity. Does can come into estrus at any time, and fawns may be born at any time of year.

Fawns are born about two hundred days after breeding. The mother's nutrition during gestation determines how many offspring are born and their health. Older, better-nourished mothers are much more likely to drop twin fawns, which can weigh from six to nine pounds (2¾–4 kg) each. Single fawns of twelve pounds (5½ kg) are not uncommon. Occasionally triplets are born during good times and ideal range conditions. Lack of adequate cover, abandonment by mothers, predators, and a host of parasites and bacterial diseases all take a toll and limit fawn survival, some years to as much as 50 percent. But this is an extremely prolific, successful, and adaptable species, more abundant today than ever, so even these losses do not threaten the general population of whitetails.

The best evidence of the whitetail's success is its great geographic range. Not even the widespread red deer of Eurasia live or once lived in so many different kinds of habitats as our whitetail.

*Above:* A male ruffed grouse drums on a forest log soon after daybreak in May to attract females. Grouse are widespread residents in big game country, especially in deer country. *Left:* Autumn, and the approach of the hunting season everywhere, seems to make whitetail bucks even more alert and suspicious than during other seasons.

# MULE DEER

## *The Great Deer of the Far West*

Every year during June in the Rocky Mountains, mule deer does gradually drift away from the herds with which they have spent the winter. If their young of the past year try to follow, does may vigorously drive them away. Eventually each doe will find a secluded area with thick cover, away from her friends, and soon will give birth to one or twin spotted fawns.

On their first day of life, each healthy fawn weighs about eight pounds (3½ kg). At birth and for a while thereafter, the fawns are easy prey for coyotes and cougars, for bears and bobcats. Their spotted coats help them to blend into their backgrounds at this perilous time. After the young have nursed and gained enough strength to coordinate their long, spindly legs, does lead the wobbly offspring a good distance away from where they were born to hide them. If twins, the fawns are hidden separately.

For at least a week, and maybe for as long as a month, the mother appears to abandon her young while she spends long hours feeding on the season's new green vegetation. She returns at intervals during the day and night to nurse the fawns. Eventually the young ones are able to follow their mother everywhere and gradually to sample whatever vegetation she is eating. Throughout their vast range, mule deer are known to eat some seven hundred different plants, grasses, forbs, brush, and small trees.

While muley fawns everywhere are rapidly gaining strength and body size, their fathers are far away, often at higher elevations, growing new antlers instead of putting on pounds. Back in December or January, after the rutting season, bucks shed their antlers. As hormone levels increase during the lengthening daylight hours of April, new antlers begin to grow from the pedicles on their skulls. The growth continues throughout the summer when living is the easiest.

*Luck—or the lack of it—plays a great part in wildlife photography just as it does in hunting. This mule deer buck appeared at daybreak just a few feet from where the authors were camped in Alberta.*

The does teach survival skills to the fawns by their own example: They are always on the alert for danger and eventually rejoin their herds for the added security of numbers. Meanwhile, the males do little except feed and doze while chewing their cud. Most of the bucks' feeding is concentrated in the cooler hours of mornings and evenings. Middays, they normally are found in the shadows, high up where they can watch the world far below. Bucks probably travel little during this time of plenty and even less during wet summers or when the morning's dew is heavy. If the season is dry, however, they may have to find drinking water every few days. Mule deer do not require as much water as often as many other big game species.

There is another hormonal change late every August. Simultaneously, the antlers harden and the velvet covering dries. By early September the velvet will have fallen away or have been rubbed off. Biologists have concluded that from this point onward the greatest weight gain for all mule deer takes place. Now the does have weaned their fawns, and all the nutrients from what they eat, in excess of daily energy needs, are converted to body fat. With antlers no longer growing, bucks also add body fat. A striking species to see at any time, mule deer are never more sleek and handsome than when quaking aspen leaves begin changing from green to yellow.

## Mule Deer Characteristics

A mule deer, *Odocoileus hemionus*, is easily distinguished from whitetails by its larger ears, resembling a mule's, by its narrow, black-tipped tail, dark gray coat, and white or light tan rump patches. Authorities generally agree that there are eleven subspecies of mule deer; blacktailed deer count for two of the subspecies. The range of all the subspecies covers most of temperate North America from the central Mexican highlands and Baja California northward to southeastern Alaska and southern Yukon, and from the Pacific Ocean eastward to a line between Saskatchewan and west Texas.

The Rocky Mountain mule deer, *O.h. hemionus*, inhabits by far the greatest range and is the largest of all the subspecies. Adults average about 130 pounds (58½ kg) for females and 250 pounds (112½ kg) for males.

The antler conformation of the mule deer differs from a whitetail's and any other antlered animal's in that the main beams branch into two beams in a Y-shape and each of these branches again in two. Normally the antler mass of a Rocky Mountain mule deer

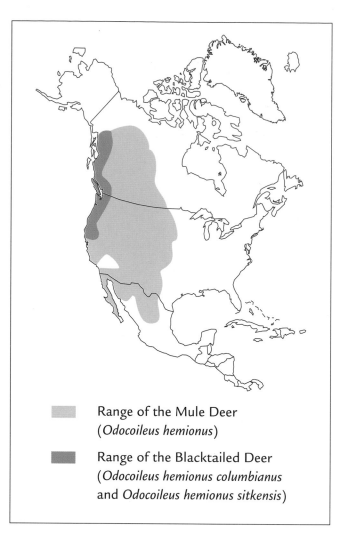

Range of the Mule Deer
(*Odocoileus hemionus*)

Range of the Blacktailed Deer
(*Odocoileus hemionus columbianus*
and *Odocoileus hemionus sitkensis*)

*Adult front hoof length: Approximately 3 inches (75 mm)
Distance between tracks when walking: Approximately 20 inches (500 mm)*

Track of the Mule Deer (*Odocoileus hemionus*) and Blacktailed Deer (*Odocoileus hemionus columbianus* and *Odocoileus hemionus sitkensis*)

**Facing page, top:** *This male Rocky Mountain muley, sleek and fat from a summer of high living, is now intent on following the trail of a doe coming into estrus.* **Facing page, bottom:** *The rut has ended here in northern Wyoming. Bucks and does still bask together on a rare sunny day as a severe winter begins.*

*Above: In Alberta, the aspen leaves are turning yellow. Bachelor friends in summer, these mule deer bucks will soon become serious rivals and temporary enemies.* **Facing page:** *Toward the end of November, this fine muley buck rests as the breeding season comes to an end. Now body weight lost during the rut must be replenished before the onset of winter.*

(but not of the coastal blacktail) is greater than that of a whitetail of similar age.

Even more distinctive is the mule deer's response to danger. Whenever it is threatened or just feels at risk, a whitetail usually bounds away immediately. The whitetail depends on speed to escape. But the mule deer reacts more deliberately by stotting on stiff legs, a maneuver that seems slower but is better suited for travel over the rough ground that muleys ordinarily inhabit. Thus, it substitutes negotiating difficult terrain for speed alone to avoid trouble. This strategy is responsible for the common belief among some hunters that mule deer are less intelligent than whitetails.

Some of the largest mule bucks I have ever met, bucks that have survived many hunting seasons, were those encountered while hunting the loftiest mountain ridges for bighorn sheep. When flushed, these animals were sure-footed enough to bound over and around difficult obstacles just like sheep.

The Rocky Mountain subspecies is equally at home in Utah's rugged Redrock country, on the grassy Great Plains, and in the Great Basin west of the Rockies. But in recent times its range apparently is shrinking as whitetails gradually expand westward by working farther up major waterways into what historically has been mule deer country. Not too many years ago, for example, whitetails began following the Missouri and then the Yellowstone River upstream until now they often are seen not far from Yellowstone Park. Where we live in the Paradise Valley of the Yellowstone, muleys abounded and whitetails were rarities before 1970. Today almost all the deer I see daily from my office window are whitetails.

Both the California mule deer, *O.h. californicus*, and the desert mule deer, *O.h. crooki*, are smaller and have more reddish coats than does the Rocky Mountain deer, but otherwise they are indistinguishable outside of a laboratory.

*The early snowfall does not discourage this Alberta buck from pursuing estrus does on a cold mountain slope.*

*A mule deer buck rests in a snowy day bed after a busy rutting season. Survival will be difficult in the harsh Rocky Mountain winter that will soon arrive.*

## Trophy Antlers

Tracking mule deer to photograph has taken us deep into some of the most magnificent real estate on the continent. There we have also met many of the animals that occasionally prey on them: mountain lions and grizzlies, black bears and wolverines. It is difficult to judge antler size from just a brief glimpse of a buck's rack, but I am convinced that two of the largest muleys we have ever seen we encountered while we were day-packing in Wyoming's Grand Teton National Park. One of these sightings took place on a gray November morning as we climbed a steep trail from White Grass Ranger Station toward Death Canyon. We were not far

underway, and a light snow was beginning to fall, when Peggy paused to look more closely at the unusually large deer tracks in soft earth beside the trail. Scanning all around, I spotted an animal high on a slope to our right. It was watching its own back trail.

For several moments we could see only the deer's massive body and swollen neck, as the antlers were hidden by spruce boughs. When the buck slowly began to move away, we could suddenly see that the antler beams were as thick as my forearms and the rack was extremely high and widespread. I fumbled for the camera in my backpack and retrieved it in time to shoot a couple of exposures. Later, although the image on the developed film was small and not really sharp, we knew this was a super buck, probably the largest muley head we had ever seen outside a trophy room. Although we practically haunted that same area every day throughout the following weeks, we never glimpsed that buck again.

A year later, also in November, and later in the day along the switch-backed trail into Granite Canyon that is popular with summertime hikers, we encountered another huge buck not far from where we had seen that first one. Our pictures taken in failing light revealed that this one also was massive and had drop points on both sides. That buck never appeared again either, although we were ready on future visits with cameras loaded with fast film. Still, these two brief experiences suggested that bucks tend to grow more massive antlers in some localities—often limited localities—than others where hunting pressure is lighter.

As if to confirm the theory, a hiker later found a heavy antler in the same vicinity but just outside Grand Teton Park. He measured and scored the half rack and came to the realization that if this antler still was connected to the animal's skull, with an antler of equal size on the opposite side, it would easily have qualified for listing in the *Boone and Crockett Records of North American Big Game* book.

## Mule Deer Through the Seasons

Maybe even more so than with whitetails, mule deer activity is concentrated during early mornings and from late afternoon until dark or beyond. Daytimes are spent bedded down in cover or the edge of cover, often in mottled shade that provides good concealment. An ideal bedding area is one with an open view all around and below, which usually means on a slope, but with an escape route behind the deer. Day in and day out, the best way to find mule deer out in the open is to rise early and stay out late. The only exception to that rule comes in late fall when the annual rut begins and most of the deer, but especially the males, are busy and moving all day long. I believe that rutting muleys also may be active throughout the night. Several times while camping during the mating season, we've heard the grunting and rattling of antlers not far outside our tent.

Mule deer bucks do not gather harems, but instead freelance their way around and among the females as they come into estrus. Early in the season, younger bucks engage in a lot of dueling. The older, more dominant males avoid this expenditure of energy; they show

their superiority with intimidation, posturing, and a blatant display of body and antler size. The eager young males spend a lot more time sparring with rivals than actually breeding. Scent glands that are located on the hind legs of muleys are activated by the rut, and these make it easy for animals ready to breed to find one another. When the breeding season finally dwindles down, leaving just faint scents lingering on brush, all of the does will have been impregnated.

When and where the ratio of bucks to does in a territory is low, biologists have noted an especially strong urge to breed among females. Even though the enthusiasm of the larger bucks may wane toward the end of the season from sheer fatigue, the fervor of unmated does increases. Late one rutting season in Yellowstone, I saw a Rocky Mountain doe aggressively following a buck and even trying to mount the buck, probably as a less than subtle hint of her availability.

## Blacktailed Deer

There are two blacktail subspecies: the Columbian blacktail, *O.h. columbianus*, and the Sitka blacktail, *O.h. sitkensis*. Both have tails similar to a whitetail's, except that the blacktail's is black on the outside, rather than brown. Blacktails' antlers have the usual mule deer conformation, however. The Columbian blacktail lives in a strip about one hundred miles (160 km) wide along the Pacific Coast from central California north to central British Columbia. Northward from there, along the southeastern Alaskan coast and including Kodiak and Afognak Islands, is Sitka blacktail range.

It is estimated that there are about two million Columbian blacktails and probably half again as many Sitka blacktails living in their restricted coastal ranges today. But we know a lot less about them than about any other North American deer. Their shy and secretive nature, their ability to skulk and blend silently into their lush green, damp environment makes them much more difficult to study than Rocky Mountain deer. I can guarantee that they are a lot harder to photograph.

Hunters always have a hard time believing that all deer have small brains in relation to body size and are not as smart as many other creatures that share their vast range. Instinct and keener senses rather than intelligence have enabled deer to survive over the centuries. But blacktails appear to be somewhat better learners than other hoofed animals. Mammal behaviorists believe that slightly larger brains give them the

edge in coping with danger and avoiding the humans that are becoming ever more numerous in blacktail country. Fortunately, blacktails are also prolific. Studies have shown that only five or six males are needed in a herd of a hundred or more to assure that all the does bear fawns in the spring.

Southeastern Alaska's Sitka blacktail almost can be classified as a marine species. These furtive, reddish deer spend most of their lives within sight of saltwater. In summer, they look out onto the sea from misty mountainsides; in winter, many migrate right down to the saltwater's edge where they live on the coarse grasses that grow just beyond high tide. They share this range year round with Alaskan brown bears and are even somewhat dependent on them. Ancient bear trails provide blacktails with the best of all travel routes through the dense evergreen forests. Many deer browse plants that grow along these pathways originate from the seeds left in piles of bear scat. In return, the brownies will eat a certain number of spotted fawns each spring.

Maybe the most interesting thing about the mule and blacktailed deer clan is that somewhere in North America their range overlaps the range of all other big game species except two, muskoxen and polar bears.

*Above:* Shy and wild, a Sitka blacktail deer races across a clear-cut forest to reach the sanctuary of a dark evergreen woods, where it will feel more secure. ***Right:*** A Columbian blacktail buck pauses before bolting into the dense, damp evergreen forest of the Northwest that is its natural environment.

# ELK

## *Monarch of the High Forest*

On a frosty dawn in mid-September, there was a skim of ice on the water bucket outside our van. We were parked in the public campground at Mammoth, northern Yellowstone, eating breakfast inside the vehicle. We had not slept well because of the noisy rutting activities of elk all around us throughout the night. Now two young males that were being kept away from the herd by the harem bull were taking out their frustrations on one another only a few yards away. We had the sound of crashing antlers to go with second mugs of coffee. Where else but in the world's first national park would this be possible?

Soon the autumn sun was high enough to flood the campground where all the campers were by now wide awake. Many were outside their tents, aiming cameras at the animals, but that made no difference to the elk. The young bulls continued to spar. The much larger harem bull, his body steaming from the exertion, squealed, snorted, bugled, and was continually on the move to prevent about twenty-four cows from wandering too far away. It was an astounding performance. We have traveled around the world to photograph wildlife, but always are drawn back to this one spot every fall, just fifty miles (80 km) from home. It is one of nature's finest spectacles.

*Cervus canadensis*, or *Cervus elaphus* as some call it, is another of our big game species that migrated to the New World from Asia. The species almost certainly originated in Tibet and western China and dispersed in all directions from there. Those that went west became the red deer of Europe and western Asia. Those going southward became the barasingas of India. And the animals that migrated eastward crossed the now non-existent Bering Sea land bridge into North America and became the six subspecies of American elk, or wapiti.

*In the first light of morning, this fine bull elk pauses at the edge of dense timber. It is fall, and the bull is beginning to assemble a harem of cows.*

When Europeans first reached North America, elk was the most widespread of all our big game species except for the cougar. That original range included most of the United States and southern Canada, with the exception of the Gulf Coast region, the Great Basin of Nevada and Utah, and probably most of New England.

One subspecies, Merriam's elk, *C.c. merriami*, originally of Arizona and northern Texas, is extinct. Another, *C.c. manitobensis*, the Manitoban elk, is today restricted to small populations in central Manitoba and Saskatchewan, but appears to be safe. Smallest in body size of all is the once-widespread Tule elk, *C.c. nannodes*, of west-central California, which exists in a few herds in the Kern River valley and at Point Reyes.

By far the most abundant is *C.c. nelsoni*, the Rocky Mountain elk. This subspecies also has the widest range, extending from the mountains of Arizona and New Mexico to Yukon.

Largest in average body size is the Olympic elk, or Roosevelt elk, *C.c. roosevelti*, which thrives in damp, lush coastal forests of the northwestern United States and Vancouver Island, British Columbia. Long ago this subspecies was introduced onto Afognak Island, Alaska, where it now is well established. There are small isolated herds in Michigan's lower peninsula and in northern Minnesota. Generally speaking, elk share mule deer country and vice versa.

## The Majestic Wapiti

The elk is the second largest antlered big game animal in North America, after the moose. Many outdoorspeople consider the elk the most noble and the most handsome trophy. A large male's antlers may spread more than four feet (120 cm) from tip to tip and the rack can weigh as much as sixty pounds (27 kg) when the bull is in its prime. The word "majestic" is often used when describing this species—and understandably so.

Bulls are generally judged to be mature during the autumn when they reach four and a half years old, but antlers may continue to increase in size for another two years. The typical "royal" bull is one with at least six antler points on each side. If he survives several hunt-

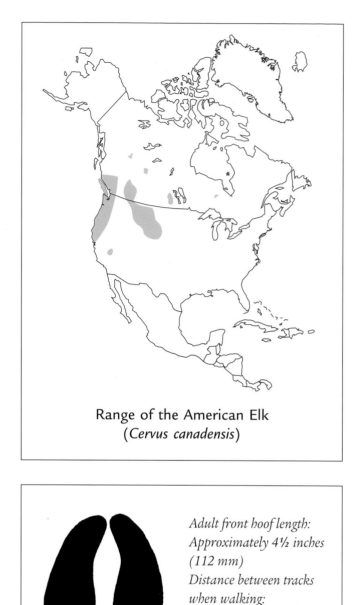

Range of the American Elk
(*Cervus canadensis*)

*Adult front hoof length: Approximately 4½ inches (112 mm)*
*Distance between tracks when walking: Approximately 24–36 inches (600–900 mm)*

Track of the American Elk (*Cervus canadensis*)

ing seasons, if the range is not too crowded or overgrazed by cattle, if genetics and nutrition are good, a bull might eventually grow antlers with seven points per side. We once photographed in Washington's Olympic National Park a magnificent Roosevelt bull

*Facing page, top: Elk inhabit some of the most spectacular real estate in western North America. This elk country is located at Bow Lake, Banff National Park, Alberta. Facing page, bottom: Cooling off in midstream, these cows in Yellowstone National Park are part of a harem attended by a master bull throughout the breeding period in September.*

*Bull elk of equal size battle head to head on a Montana mountainside. The winner will "own" the harem bedded down out of sight on the slope below.*

that carried an astonishing total of fifteen points. It was still in the velvet when we saw it in late August.

That Olympic male, we judged, stood about five feet (150 cm) at the shoulder and might have weighed well over 800 pounds (360 kg). Studies that took place over several years at the National Elk Refuge in Jackson, Wyoming, give us more reliable dimensions and weights for the Rocky Mountain subspecies, about eight thousand of which spend winters there. Adult cows weighed from 450 to almost 600 pounds (200–270 kg). Bulls weighed from 500 to almost 800 pounds (225–360 kg). To maintain so large a body size an elk must eat, year in and year out, more than four times as much as a whitetailed deer of the same age.

The North American elk must be classified as a herd or gregarious species, although the degree of the herding varies from season to season. Mature bulls remain apart from cow and calf herds most of the year, but most males form their own, much smaller bach-

elor herds. During the calving season, normally the month of June, the cows scatter widely into small groups all across their summer range. But once the spotted calves are strong enough to travel far, the females gather into ever larger groups. These herds remain largely intact until the next calving season.

The coats of elk are light-brown to reddish-brown in color in the summer and fall with darker heads and legs but always with light tan rump patches; the coats gradually turn grayish in winter. Both sexes seem heavier in the body and sturdier in physique than do mule deer and whitetails. Shy and suspicious of people and animal predators, they have tremendous vitality and thrive in many of America's largest intact wilderness areas. At the same time, elk living in sanctuaries such as Yellowstone and Banff and Jasper National Parks in Alberta, where they are not hunted, often become so tolerant of people that they become a nuisance, occasionally even a menace.

*A powerful old bull bugles on a fall morning, advertising his availability to breed. His bugling is not meant to challenge rival bulls as is widely believed.*

## Elk Characteristics

The late naturalist and wilderness advocate Olaus Murie began studying elk in several locations during the 1940s. He always was especially interested in what elk ate. Since then, many other biologists have studied elk diets and the conclusion of all is about the same: Elk eat almost every plant that grows, native or introduced. However, the elk herds living on one mountain range might subsist largely on plants that do not even grow on another range nearby. When the number of elk increases beyond the carrying capacity of its range, that range becomes seriously overbrowsed and overgrazed, after which the health of the elk and other animals in the area deteriorates. In extreme instances, some die of starvation.

Of all North American big game, only caribou annually travel greater distances every year. It is true that some populations of elk scarcely move at all between winter and summer, but most make migrations twice each year from higher summer ranges to lower winter ranges and back again. Summers are spent in green meadows that may be thousands of feet in elevation above the valley winter ranges. Some elk herds in western Wyoming also travel considerable distances laterally. For example, animals that spend summer in southern Yellowstone Park make their regular late fall trek eighty miles (128 km) or more to the National Elk Refuge in Wyoming.

During recent decades, much of the elk's traditional winter range has evaporated as people build towns, cattle ranches, roads, and ski resorts along or across old migration routes. Our elk herds have been saved only by creating elk feeding grounds (such as the National Elk Refuge, which is the largest) where the wintering herds are provided with hay and food pellets to sustain them through the "hunger moon."

Elk become more susceptible to such diseases as necrotic stomatitis, scabies, and a number of other

parasites when they are concentrated by the hundreds, sometimes the thousands, on confined wintering areas. This is also the time of year when some elk inevitably wander into towns and get into all kinds of trouble, including eating ornamental shrubbery around suburban homes, getting entangled in and tearing up fences and clotheslines, walking across schoolyards during recess, and running into cars. In Jackson, Wyoming, a cow elk was found eating potato chips out of the back end of a parked delivery truck. She even followed the truck for some distance into traffic as it was driven away. Another cow found sleeping in a Jackson motel parking lot charged the custodian who tried to shoo her away.

As a species, elk are extraordinary survivors. Many elk hunters know how well and how far a seriously wounded animal can travel. During the 1960s in Yellowstone's Madison River meadows, we watched a large bull keep control of his harem and drive other bulls away, although he had been blinded in an earlier fight. One eyeball was almost torn from its socket—a grisly sight—and the other eye was glazed over. I am certain that animal was depending solely on its nose and ears to maintain its position.

We have watched elk swim rivers swollen with icy snowmelt without hesitation. Once twin calves fol-

*Above:* In early June, the Lamar River is swollen by snow melt, blocking the migration of a Yellowstone elk herd to its traditional summer range in the high back country. Crossing it will be a dangerous undertaking. *Left:* In golden autumn a splendid bull elk patrols the Gardiner River valley in northern Yellowstone National Park. This is an excellent area for viewing the annual fall rut at close range.

*As summer ends, velvet peels or is rubbed from the antlers of bull elk, giving them a rakish appearance. Soon the hard, bare bone will be completely exposed.*

*On a frosty October morning in Yellowstone's Gibbon Meadow, a lone bull elk studies the photographer before coming fully into open view.*

lowed their mother into the torrent, and for a time it seemed they were doomed. As we stood some distance away, watching but not breathing, both calves were washed, struggling, and certainly deeply chilled, far downstream. But eventually both managed to regain their footing in shallower water and clamber out onto the far bank and finally join their mother.

For most elk that survive hunting seasons, life between these times is a matter of securing enough to eat. Cougars kill a few wapiti, bears hunt for elk calves, and elk herds in some areas, especially in Canada and now Yellowstone, must be alert for wolves. But given the combination of good range and decent luck, elk can live a long time. Wyoming biologists showed me the skull of a bull known from its ear tag to be an elderly ten years old. It had been killed in a car collision, but might otherwise have lived several years longer, judging from the good condition of its teeth.

Rocky Mountain elk living in captivity have survived as long as nineteen years. One bull on a northwestern game farm is known to have sired seventy calves. Probably the longevity record belongs to an elk shot in Arizona in 1937; in its ear was a metal tag placed there twenty-four years earlier when it was one year old.

Because of their great trophy value, older, bigger bulls are too often the targets of poachers, especially in national parks where the animals are comparatively tolerant of people. Yellowstone, particularly, has been a magnet for poachers, who find their dirty work much easier in times when budget cuts, courtesy of the United States Congress, reduce the park ranger force to a skeleton crew. At one point there was not a single ranger on duty in Yellowstone for one night each week, and of course it was then that the poachers boldly went to work. During the late 1990s, both professional poachers and people poaching just for the thrill of it shot a number of outstanding bull elk only short distances from park roads and passing tourists.

Shed antlers as well as the living animals are fully protected in our parks, but in 1980 rangers found a capsized inflatable raft in the Yellowstone River not far, as the crow flies, from park headquarters. When they righted the craft they were astounded to see a large pile of elk antlers securely tied to it. The boater-poacher was missing and may have drowned in that fast, cold water. But ever since, rangers have wondered how long this clever method had been used to carry how many antlers outside the park undetected.

## Rutting Battles and Bugling

Each September in elk country everywhere a phenomenon called photoperiodism triggers hormonal, and therefore behavioral, changes in the animals. In simpler words, it is the decreasing amount of daylight as summer blends into fall—and not hot or cold weather, rain, or early snow, as many believe—that determines when elk and other hoofed big game will enter the breeding period.

During an abnormally hot or dry autumn the rut may seem to be delayed, but it probably is not. Most of the action only shifts to nights rather than daytime. Elk have excellent night vision, and darkness would be no hindrance to their activities. Somehow, almost all of the cows in a given area are bred during the same period, year after year. And always this breeding season is one of the most exciting times and activities to watch on the entire continent.

The thing that most symbolizes the rut and is also among the most stirring sounds in nature is the bugling of the bulls. This sound varies from animal to animal, but usually begins as a low, hoarse bellow and rises to a shrill calliope squealing or screaming that can be heard far away. The bugle ends in a series of deep gasps or grunts. No matter how often it is heard, it re-mains the most thrilling wilderness sound. Although the volume and greater intensity of bugling may often indicate whether the bugler is an old elk or a young one, it is not an absolute indication of the bull's age or size, as is widely believed. Nor can we be absolutely certain why bulls bugle.

Once observers thought that bugling was simply a challenge to other bulls, probably because the bugling period often is interrupted by fighting for dominance and control of a harem. Another theory is that a bugler is just "blowing off steam." A far more likely theory is that bugling is a form of male advertising. The bull is indicating to females that it is available and to other males that is in charge of the situation. The most powerful bulls seem to bugle the most often to emphasize these points.

Still, the annual rut is more than just a tournament of bugling. The strongest, most active, most aggressive elk (which normally, but not always, have the heaviest antlers) round up as many cows as they can manage into a harem. It requires tremendous and almost continuous effort to hold the group together and keep rival bulls, who tend to circle the edges, at a distance. Often a harem-breeding territory is an open, grassy meadow where cows can graze and with streams serving as boundaries. This kind of terrain makes it easier to keep track of as many as twenty-five or, rarely, even more cows. As they come into estrus, they are mounted and impregnated by the harem bull, until early in October when the rut winds down. The cows wander off and the exhausted bulls rest and once again eat to regain strength needed for the coming winter. But the seed for another generation of elk has been planted.

# MOOSE

## *The Elusive Giant*

The citizens of Anchorage, Alaska, are normally blasé about wildlife and wildlife encounters. After all, an estimated three hundred moose as well as other creatures spend their winters within the city limits—and they sometimes wear out their welcome. But during the winter of 1994–1995, the in-town moose population more than tripled, to about one thousand. Almost seven feet (2 meters) of snow fell in the surrounding mountains, driving the animals down into Anchorage streets and into suburban backyards in search of food. Not all human residents welcomed them.

One moose wandered onto the city's University of Alaska campus and trampled a man to death after being taunted by beer-guzzling students. Elsewhere the visiting moose charged people and kicked a few yapping dogs that tried to haze them out of gardens. It was an intense winter all around that ended none too soon when the moose retreated to their regular haunts behind the rapidly melting snows of spring.

Moose also were making news thousands of miles from Alaska. In Ontario, one cow learned that the sound of a chain saw could be considered the tolling of a dinner bell. Whenever she heard firewood cutters out sawing, she would race to the spot and eat the small limbs that crashed to the ground. Eventually, forester Frankie Gagnon found himself cutting browse especially for his dark and docile friend.

*With stringers of velvet hanging from its wide palmate antlers, a central Alaska moose travels toward a traditional courting and breeding ground, where it will compete with other bulls for the cows also gathered there.*

A pack of house dogs chased a yearling moose out onto the ice of Conception Bay, Newfoundland; when a small ice floe broke away and drifted out to sea, the moose was stranded on it. Fortunately, someone spotted the yearling before it floated from sight, and provincial wildlife officials called for a helicopter. With difficulty the chopper crew harnessed the frightened moose and air-lifted the four-hundred-pound (180-kg) animal to a nearby woods, where it was released. The yearling calmly walked away, somehow maintaining the dignity all moose seem to possess.

## Moose Characteristics

I first saw a moose decades ago in Ontario, and it was a shock to me. It seemed a preposterous, clumsy, and magnificent creature all at the same time. I didn't realize then that here, this species wading in Nipigon Lake, was the largest member of the world's deer family. I judged it to stand six feet (180 cm) at the withers and I especially remember the bell, or dewlap, hanging from its neck. At the time, I thought the animal's antlers, covered with dark velvet, were massive, but I realized later that I had been looking at only an average Canadian moose rack—if that. But it made a lasting impression on this young man.

Some moose are a lot heavier and grow much larger antlers than others. The Alaskan-Yukon moose, *Alces alces gigas*, might reach a ton (900 kg) in weight, measure almost eight feet (240 cm) at the shoulder, and on its massive head carry a set of antlers that spreads six feet (180 cm) from tip to tip and weighs up to eighty-five pounds (38 kg). A male moose can grow as much pure bone in its antlers in just three months as a human skeleton grows to reach its maximum size over a period of eighteen years. Moose may grow an inch (2½ cm) of antler per day.

The three other recognized subspecies of moose are smaller than the Alaska-Yukon race. *A.a. americana*, the eastern moose, is found from northern New England to Labrador. The Manitoban moose, *A.a. andersoni*, ranges across Canada from Quebec to British Columbia. The smallest race of the world's largest deer is *A.a. shirasi*, the Wyoming or Shiras moose, which lives in the northern Rocky Mountains as far south as Colo-

Range of the Moose (*Alces alces*)

*Adult front hoof length: Approximately 7 inches (175 mm)*
*Distance between tracks when walking: Approximately 24–60 inches (600–1500 mm)*

Track of the Moose (*Alces alces*)

rado. It was named after the pioneer wildlife photographer and conservationist, George Shiras III, who made some of the first and finest black and white pictures of the species. This is also the species Peggy and I watched progress from birth until old age just outside

*Facing page, top:* A calf follows its mother across a shallow bay of Wonder Lake in Denali National Park, Alaska. The park contains much excellent moose habitat. *Facing page, bottom:* Constantly alert for danger from any side, a cow moose feeds at dusk on the nutritious green vegetation growing in an Alaskan beaver pond.

92

93

our windows when we lived for many years in Jackson Hole.

The palmate antlers of all four subspecies are similar, except for one thing. Antlers of forest-dwelling Shiras bulls tend to curve upward and higher above the skull to make travel through timber easier. The antlers of Alaska-Yukon bulls, on the other extreme, have evolved to grow straight out from the skull for easier carriage in more windy, open habitat.

No matter where it lives and no matter what a person's first impression of it, a moose is not a clumsy beast. Those long legs are pistons that allow it to travel almost effortlessly over dense deadfalls and to plow through belly-deep snow that would trap other big game species. The large split hooves splay enough to make passage through soft mud and slush almost as easy as on hard ground. One moose can bound through the woods as noisily as a whole terrified herd, or it can slip away as silently as a ghost, whichever route instinct suggests is the best way to go.

The moose of all four subspecies spend much of their lives close to water, in riparian zones, river bottoms, marshlands, beaver ponds, and usually smaller, shallow lakes. All of these are habitats where the willows and other aquatic vegetation that moose prefer are easily available throughout the summer. They may

*Above: Beavers and their dam-building are extremely important to big game such as moose, which thrive around beaver ponds. Bears catch beavers and eat them when they can. **Right:** Mt. Moran is the backdrop for a Shiras, or Wyoming moose, about to cross the Snake River in Grand Teton National Park.*

*Above:* Willow leaves are a mainstay of a moose's diet in central Alaska. Although still young, this bull already carries massive antlers still in velvet. *Facing page:* With antlers still covered in velvet in late summer, a Yukon moose cautiously crosses a meadow where a wolf pack had howled the night before.

not stray far from such soggy places at any other season. Still, we have been surprised occasionally to find moose high up on mountainsides, both in summer and fall, and far from any wetlands. That is especially true of the Wyoming moose, which may live within a ten-mile (16-km) radius of where it was born, as long as the food supply lasts.

The early settlers in North America called the moose "elk," as it was known in Europe. The origin of the word "moose" isn't clear, but it probably is a Native American word now believed to mean "twig-eater." In any case, moose are twig-eaters, browsing on the tender tips, buds, and leaves of many trees and shrubs, especially on the many varieties of willow. An adult moose can easily strip the leaves of a willow from ground level to about ten feet (3 meters) high. A moose can eat a tenth of its body weight each day during the summer months, converting a lot of it to fat. Thus, a half-ton (450-kg) bull may consume one hundred pounds (45 kg) daily. Young moose may add two to

five pounds (1–2¼ kg) in body weight per summer day.

Moose are also grazers, both on land and in the water. They gorge on new green grass by spreading their front legs wide apart or even by kneeling down. Or they wade, sometimes in water so deep that it almost covers them, to better reach aquatic plants.

Next to its great body, the oversized muzzle may be a moose's most distinctive feature. But the prehensile lip is necessary to feed selectively on roots, reeds, and tubers it finds under water. Wading flank-deep, a moose can feed with its eyes just above the surface, watching for approaching danger as it eats submerged vegetation.

The driver of a road grader told me of an incident he witnessed while maintaining the gravel highway that winds across Denali Park in Alaska. A cow and calf moose were feeding peacefully in a beaver pond and, except for eyes and ears, both were totally submerged and preoccupied. Then, for no apparent reason, both suddenly seemed to explode out of the water and kept

*Above:* A cow moose greets a still, sub-zero dawn in the Buffalo Valley of Grand Teton National Park—excellent Wyoming moose range. *Right:* Trout Creek in Yellowstone's Hayden Valley is a mirror for a young Shiras bull in early summer. The moose shares this area with herds of bison and passing grizzly bears.

running until they were out of sight in dense alder brush. Moments later the grader operator saw the reason for the hasty exit: A large grizzly bear was ambling toward the pond. The moose obviously were aware of its approach, perhaps even before the bear knew of their presence in the water.

At times the senses of a moose may seem less keen than those of a deer, maybe because deer always bound away at top speed. But the moose's hearing, vision, and scenting ability are certainly adequate. It simply takes a greater danger to frighten a moose than a deer.

## Moose Through the Seasons

Besides the powerful body, a healthy moose carries a heavy blanket of hair that varies in color from dark brown to black. Its legs are lighter colored, usually gray. There is an undercoat of fine wool beneath the long outer hair that enables a moose to withstand the bitterest of winters by minimizing loss of body heat. In summer, the wool protects against the mosquitoes and black flies that swarm in moose habitat.

At the onset of spring, moose gradually shed their long and graying outer coat, revealing a body much leaner than in fall. For a time, all moose appear mangy, or desperately ill, but quickly a glossy new coat replaces the winter-damaged old one. Long hours of busy feeding soon rounds out the body contours. In late May or June, after a gestation of about eight months, cows retreat into the most secluded places and give birth to single calves or, occasionally, to twins.

It is an understatement to say that there is a strong bond between cows and calves. Moose may not be as protective of space or territory as are many other wild creatures, but cows surely are protective of their young. In fact, a large percentage of the incidents of moose attacking people every year are cases of females defending calves, rather than bulls attacking those who venture too close, as one would expect. Cows seem to go especially after small, annoying dogs. But in wilderness areas that they share with wolves, it is difficult for an adult moose to save a calf from an experienced hunting pack.

Not surprisingly, some of the most exciting times we have spent watching and photographing moose have occurred during the rut. Rutting males are at their most imposing and most belligerent during this period, but I do not believe that they are any more dangerous to humans, as is often stated, as long as humans give them enough maneuvering room. But as soon as the brown velvet peels and hangs from red-stained, fully hardened antlers, every encounter between two bulls of similar size is automatically one of rivalry.

Completely uninterested in food now, bulls begin the search for females. They wander far, grunt a lot, slash young trees and brush with antlers, and stare at the world with antagonistic, red-rimmed eyes. When two or more bulls meet in the presence of cows, if posturing to signal dominance doesn't work, there usually is a good bit of head-to-head fighting. Perhaps because of the palmate shape of the antlers, there seem to be fewer serious injuries from what surely is the noisiest fighting of any North American big game animals. As with all other big game species, the most powerful males emerge victorious and do most of the breeding.

Moose do not gather harems. Rather, a cow coming into estrus might attract a number of males—I once saw six—that follow her every move, with the largest bull always the closest and the smallest suitors bringing up the hopeful rear. When the rut ends and the skies are heavy and gray with snow, all the bulls are much thinner and wearier than when the rut began. That will make it much more difficult to survive until spring, particularly if the snows fall early, before they can replenish their energy reserves.

Of all North American deer, moose are the least gregarious, the least likely to join in herds. But neither are they solitary animals as is so often written; seldom do we see a moose alone, from birth onward. Except briefly during mating when they are surrounded by bulls, cows almost always are accompanied by calves. It appears to me that bulls also usually live in small bachelor groups, segregated by size, especially throughout winter. The largest bulls—former rivals—stay together, but apart from groups of smaller bulls. Those that live through the winter on short rations, manage to negotiate deep snows, and avoid predators will greet summer, grow fat again, and sire the next generation.

# CARIBOU

## *Splendor of the Arctic*

One of the finest and most spectacular of the several hundred national parks on earth is Denali in central Alaska. Every summer, visitors come here from around the world to see the grizzly bears and white sheep, the matchless wilderness scenes, and Mt. McKinley, highest peak on the continent. This is also the only national park in the United States where caribou can be seen living wild as they have for centuries.

The Denali caribou herd is one of about thirty that inhabit Alaska and northern Canada and is far from the largest. That distinction belongs to the Western Arctic Herd that contains about 400,000 animals. But the Denali group may be the most interesting and valuable to science because it is the only one anywhere that lives its entire life cycle without any human hunting pressure. Also, all of the other animal species that lived here before Alaska was "discovered" are still present. So we have here that rare ecosystem of Denali National Park and Preserve that remains entirely intact. It is a northern nature laboratory without equal as the twentieth century ends.

There are four subspecies of the caribou, *Rangifer tarandus*, inhabiting the northernmost land areas of North America. Baffin caribou, *R.t. groenlandicus*, lives on Greenland, Baffin Island, and much of the vast region from Hudson Bay north to the Arctic Ocean. The little-known white caribou, or Peary's caribou, *R.t. pearyi*, ranges over the northernmost islands of Canada in the Arctic Ocean. The woodland caribou, *R.t. caribou*, is a threatened animal that lives in scattered evergreen forests almost completely across southern Canada, with a small number clinging to existence in northern Idaho. The barren ground caribou of Denali and the rest of Alaska is *R.t. granti*. For antler record-keeping purposes, the Boone and Crockett club recognizes a fifth subspecies, the mountain caribou, *R.t. osborni*, of mountainous western Canada.

*Mature barren ground caribou bulls carry majestic antlers, especially in relation to their modest body size. They use them as weapons during sometimes savage rutting duels for dominance.*

## Caribou Characteristics

Except for Peary's caribou, which are pale gray or cream-colored, all the subspecies are similar in appearance. A long, gray-haired coat with thick, fine wool underneath insulates their bodies so well (with no increase in metabolism required to maintain body temperature) that caribou keep warm even when Arctic temperatures are far below freezing. Muzzles are furred (except around the nostrils) to keep the caribou's face warm when it probes in snow for food.

Besides the efficient hair coat, caribou also have a backup system to maintain a normal body temperature of 105° F (40.5° C) that is similar to that of Arctic waterfowl and in the flippers of marine mammals. Blood vessels that carry warm blood from the heart to the legs lie close beside the vessels returning cold blood to the heart. These heat exchangers keep the animal's legs well above freezing.

Caribou are equipped with hooves ideal for their lifestyle. They are large, measuring five by five inches (12½x12½ cm) on adult males, and change somewhat to adapt to different seasons. Walking on the solid, sometimes rocky ground of summer rounds off the hard edges and makes movement a little easier. But after snow again covers northern Canada, the hoof's hard outer edge grows back and into a concave shape. This gives better traction on packed snow and ice. It is also better for pawing and digging in snow for food.

Both females and males have antlers, although the cows' are smaller. There are some herds, such as the Ungava herd in eastern Canada, in which many cows are always antlerless. But there are few animals in the American wilderness more impressive than fully grown caribou bulls with white manes blowing in the autumn wind, displaying scarlet antlers from which the velvet has just peeled. When you spot such an animal against a fall landscape of red and gold, the result is breathtaking.

A mature bull's antlers may grow to over three feet (90 cm) high, with long, semi-palmate beam ends containing multiple—up to forty—points, with flattened brow tines or "shovels" that extend straight out above the face. Like whitetails, elk, and moose, caribou bulls use their hardened antlers for "bragging," or flaunting, during the increasing tempo of the annual rut. They also use them in loud, violent clashes with rival males of similar size. It is not unusual for several bull fights to break out at once on the crowded breeding grounds near the end of fall migration close to wintering areas.

Range of the Caribou (*Rangifer tarandus*)

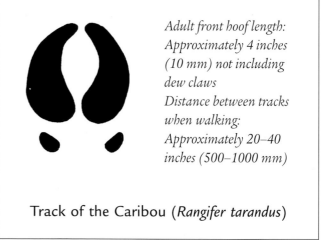

*Adult front hoof length: Approximately 4 inches (10 mm) not including dew claws*
*Distance between tracks when walking: Approximately 20–40 inches (500–1000 mm)*

Track of the Caribou (*Rangifer tarandus*)

Often the breeding takes place while the whole herd is still migrating.

## Caribou Through the Seasons

The life of a barren ground caribou is almost a continual migration from traditional spring calving areas to wintering areas and back again. To an extent, these movements are predictable, each herd following the same trails and often even the same tracks they used before humans began to hunt and subsist on them.

**Above:** *Through low-lying fall mists, bachelor barren ground bulls begin the trek toward breeding grounds in the Alaska Range, following old, familiar trails.* **Left:** *Mountain ranges are only minor obstacles to migrating herds of barren ground caribou. This band of cows and calves was photographed near Bathurst Inlet, Northwest Territories.*

*Two handsome barren ground bulls pause on the Alaskan tundra. It is late summer, and biting insects now are few. The weather is still mild. In a few weeks the annual rut will begin.*

*In little more than three summer months, this barren ground caribou bull has grown a heavy set of antlers. Now it stands majestically in early autumn Alaskan color.*

Each herd also makes these great journeys at roughly the same time each year, a fact that has helped primitive as well as modern hunters intercept them. The start of spring migration probably is triggered by increasing daylight and physiological changes taking place in females. But scientists such as Canada's George Calef, who has spent many years studying caribou, still admits to being puzzled by some aspects of migration. For example, how important is weather and snow depth? Why don't all barren ground herds everywhere begin their migrations at the same time?

Spring migrations may be the most critical. From more sheltered wintering areas, often below the timberline (the undulating line that extends across Canada, marking the northernmost limit of tree growth), these treks aim toward open tundra where there is enough to eat during the crucial calving season. No area in the entire Arctic exists with enough nutritious vegetation to support herds of large mammals concentrated there year round. Spring migrations are led by females, maybe by the oldest and best navigators, or maybe by those feeling the most urgent need to find a suitable place to drop her calf. They travel about ten to twenty miles (16–32 km) each day. Calef writes that forty-mile (64-km) "dashes" are not uncommon, over everything from still frozen lakes and snowpacks to rocky ridges and mostly spongy tundra, almost always following the path of least resistance. Traveling in parallel single-file lines

*A woodland caribou bull browses its way through its cool, evergreen habitat. Few of this species survive south of the Canadian border.*

makes the going easier for the herd. Bulls bring up the rear—sometimes the distant rear—after dawdling longer in the wintering areas.

Barren ground caribou everywhere must keep moving in order not to overgraze any vital part of their range. They feed en masse at dusk and daybreak, resting and ruminating during the middle of the day, and then move on. Quite often wolves accompany them on their travels, picking off stragglers. Over winter the animals lose from 10 to 20 percent of their body weight, mostly from fat reserves in body cavities and along the saddle. There is great competition in the herd for available food, and weaker members slowly starve and are eaten by wolves.

As with elk and some other big game, the rut takes an especially heavy toll on the bulls, which eat little during that season. As fat is used up and glycogen stores are depleted, males develop a rank odor and unpleasant taste. Native American hunters knew that old bulls were inedible after the rut and did not pursue them. Therefore, in winter, with the bulls' energy at a low ebb, the strongest cows become the dominant members of the herd, using their hooves and antlers when necessary to secure food for themselves and their own calves.

The life cycle of the woodland caribou is somewhat different from that of the barren ground herds. They usually are more sedentary, traveling far less because it is not necessary. Movement is more vertical than across vast distances. Males stand about four feet (120 cm) tall at the shoulder and weigh from 250 to 400 pounds (112½–180 kg). Females weigh 150 to 250 pounds (67½–112½ kg). They spend winters in hemlock-cedar forests and summers on isolated ridges free of human encroachment.

## Conserving the Caribou

During one of my early trips to Denali, in the late 1950s, biologist Adolph Murie told me that he estimated the park herd at ten thousand animals, based on road counts during the spring and fall migrations. That estimate may have been on the high side. Twenty years later, researcher Will Troyer believed that only about 1,200 animals still wandered the park, an alarming decline of almost 90 percent. Caribou elsewhere in Alaska had also declined to the same degree, but this was blamed on over-shooting. By 1990, the Denali Park herd was back up to about four thousand animals. What caused or causes these dramatic fluctuations?

Since 1984, Denali caribou have been studied as much as tight research budgets allow. Important questions to answer were the number of calves born every year, how many survive, and for how long. That meant locating the calves as soon as possible after birth, usually using a helicopter to land nearby, running down the calf on foot, and then collaring it. The first fact the scientists learned was the most important to their success. If the calf was more than two or three days old, the fastest sprinter on the research crew could not catch it. Calves that they did catch were weighed, sexed, and examined before a radio transmitter on an elastic collar was placed around the neck. The collar, designed to stretch as the animal grew, would fall off in about a year's time.

Radio collars have been widely used to track, monitor, and study most big game animals. Transmitters allow researchers to locate and follow the movements of the animals around the clock, even when they are far away and out of sight. A whole herd of migrating elk or a single bighorn sheep can be located accurately from the radio signals. When a collar that is still on the animal remains absolutely motionless for an hour, the radio beeps signal that the animal is probably dead. This is how Denali biologists learned that, of the first 378 caribou calves collared, 171, or almost half, died before they were fifteen days old. This early calf mortality was highest during springs following severe winters. But once past that critical first fifteen days of life, caribou calves have an 80 percent chance of making it to their first birthday.

What caused the early deaths? Some perished in accidents such as drowning in icy creek crossings. The human handling may have been a factor. But predators including wolves, coyotes, golden eagles, wolverines, and especially bears were mainly responsible. Grizzly bears with cubs emerge from their winter dens at almost exactly the same time as caribou are dropping calves. Since some bears den on or near calving grounds, they are in a prime position to catch their first meal of the year nearby. Also, certain grizzlies become adept at finding caribou calves. But once a calf reaches ten days of age or so, it is unlikely that any bear can catch it.

By contrast, wolf predation seems unrelated to the age of calves. It depends far more on the ability, and perhaps luck, of the packs in finding herds of cows with calves. The odds of this happening are low in a sanctuary as large as Denali. When they do locate them, however, the wolves may kill as many as they can, consuming them over several days. The evidence suggests that young animals of any species live precarious lives until their senses and physical skills can match those of the animals that want to eat them.

Here as elsewhere, predation is not the main factor in falling or increasing herd populations. In fact, we still have no idea exactly what causes the periodic fluctuations in many wild animal populations that often concern us. In this case, barren ground caribou evolved along with their predators thousands of years ago. If we let nature take its course, they will continue to live together in acceptable balance.

Land clearing, mining, and logging have taken a terrible toll on former caribou range. Within the United States in 1987, only twenty-five to thirty woodland caribou survived in extreme northern Idaho. Despite several restockings from British Columbia's Selkirk Mountains, a census in 1993 revealed only forty to fifty at most in Idaho. Programs to reintroduce woodland caribou from Newfoundland into Maine, where they were once abundant, have also failed. The reasons cited were competition with whitetailed deer, brain worm disease (carried by whitetails, which remain symptom-free, however), and predation by black bears. Conservationists everywhere hope that rampant oil exploration in the Arctic will never have a similar effect on the barren ground caribou of Canada and Alaska.

*Above:* This Alaska caribou bull has been stalked and chased for a distance by three young wolves, but they have given up the hunt. Over open ground, healthy caribou usually can outrun their predators. *Left:* Over the ages, the gray wolf evolved with and shared the same ranges with all the animals in this book, preying on most of them. Today wolves survive mostly as symbols of our once vast big game wilderness that is too fast being lost.

# MOUNTAIN LION

## *The Ghost Cat*

A person might spend an entire lifetime outdoors in North America and never catch a glimpse of either of the two large native cats, the mountain lion and the jaguar. In fact, you might not even find sign of them while exploring the most likely cat country. Neither the mountain lion nor the jaguar is abundant, and both are extremely stealthy and secretive in their ways.

Once extending throughout the entire United States, across southern Canada, and southward through Mexico, the present range of the cougar, *Felis concolor* or "the cat of one color," has been reduced mainly to western mountain and desert regions and southwestern Texas. A small relict population of thirty to fifty survives in the Everglades and Big Cypress Swamp in southern Florida. There are enough "sightings" every year to suggest that a few may still cling to existence in eastern Canada, too. Biologists estimated the United States population at 16,000 in 1995.

This cat of one color is also the cat of many names. Most common besides *mountain lion* are *cougar, puma,* and *panther*; you also occasionally hear the names *painter* and *catamount*. Even more unprintable names are used, mostly by the ranchers who inspired the predator control programs during the early 1990s that almost wiped out the species. It is unfortunate that such a splendid animal is so widely regarded, at best, as a menace.

Fully grown male cougars measure up to nine feet (270 cm) long, including the tail; females are normally about a foot shorter. Weight varies from 80 pounds (36 kg) for a small female to almost 200 pounds (90 kg) for a large male. Although an occasional older specimen may be grayish, the common single color is tawny to reddish overall, which blends well into the natural environment.

*The "cat of one color," the cougar, or North American mountain lion, is a furtive feline seldom seen, even where it is fairly abundant.*

## The Solitary Hunter

If any one word best describes mountain lions, it is solitary. Males seek out and consort briefly with females who have come into estrus, but otherwise they are mysterious and solitary hunters. Females also always hunt alone, sometimes to feed litters of one or two to six kittens with which they do not spend a lot of time. Although cougars have lived as long as twenty years in captivity, it is a rare one that lives to half that age in the wild.

Most of the mountain lion's prey are the other big game animals. Historically, deer and lion country were one and the same. Today, deer still make up at least half of the cat's diet. A week before I sat down to write this book, a cougar killed and ate most of a whitetail less than one hundred yards (90 meters) from my window. Healthy, adult cats are able to bring down elk larger than themselves; they will also eat smaller prey such as beavers, grouse, hares, skunks, and even porcupines and mice in a pinch. Examinations of scat reveal that they will also occasionally eat green grass, which may purge parasites from their digestive tracts.

Lions locate prey by sight and hearing and, judging from evidence left in fresh snow, they may spend a lot of time watching and waiting for a deer to move closer before making their move. But some cats in certain situations slink toward a target, crouching low and moving silently, taking every advantage of available cover. The closer it gets to the deer, the more cautious the cat becomes, belly now scraping the ground, ears flattened. Finally, perhaps when the deer looks up too late, the cougar's balance shifts forward, and like a sprinter breaking out of the starting blocks, it rockets toward the deer in an explosive final rush.

If the rush is successful—and the odds of success depend on the cougar's experience and the terrain—it clutches with foreclaws at the deer's shoulder and tries to reach the neck with large, sharp canine teeth. The perfect stalk ends quickly. But cougars have been injured, at times mortally, by strong, struggling prey. Researchers have found the decaying carcasses of deer and lions together, the lion with a hoof puncturing its rib cage. Idaho biologist Maurice Hornocker, who for a long time virtually lived with lions of the Idaho Wilderness Area, once found the remains of a lion and elk

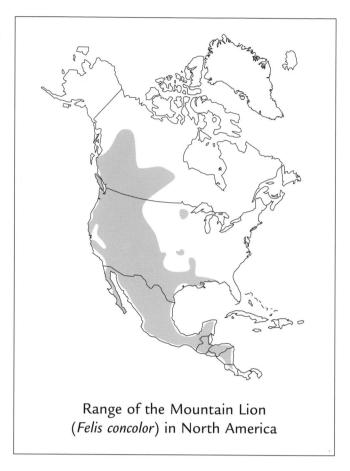

**Range of the Mountain Lion (*Felis concolor*) in North America**

*Front adult paw length: Approximately 4 inches (100 mm)*
*Distance between tracks when walking: Approximately 22 inches (550 mm)*

**Track of the Mountain Lion (*Felis concolor*) and Jaguar (*Panthera onca*)**

who had rolled down a steep mountainside together, ending with the death of both.

As it is with many large predators, life for the cougar is either feast or famine. A feast may consist of as much as ten pounds (4½ kg) of meat bolted immediately after a successful kill. Wild flesh is easily digested

*High on the list of gravely endangered American animals is the Florida panther, a southern subspecies of the mountain lion. It is making a last stand in the Everglades region.*

*Especially when coming into estrus, female cougars may be far more often heard than seen. This one is caterwauling—emitting a loud, chilling scream that can be heard far away in the night.*

*On a first foray outside their natal den, twin cougar cubs follow their mother. When their mother is out on a serious hunt, the cubs will be left behind.*

and does not require as much processing as do plant foods in the stomach. But after that banquet is consumed, weeks may pass before there is another feast. Many large predators, cougars included, probably gulp down food when they have it, before larger animals or scavengers can claim it.

## Cougars Through the Seasons

Cougars begin to breed when about two years old. Females are polyestrous, meaning they have several estrus cycles annually. When coming into season, a female wanders more widely than usual, vocalizing with squalls, whistles, maybe even screams and caterwauls,

and leaving behind a scent that a male or males soon find. Where the cougar population is low and males are scarce, an estrus period might pass without breeding. The estrus period can take place at any time of year.

Most cougar kittens in North America are born, following three months' gestation, in the period from April to July. The birthplace is always remote, beneath a tree deadfall, an undercut bank, in a rocky depression or, ideally, in a cave. Newborn kittens weigh about a pound (½ kg), are blind, and have dark body spots and dark rings on their short tails. Their eyes open at about two weeks, at which time captive kittens become playful; wild ones probably behave the same way.

*A solitary cougar stalks across the high rangelands of western Montana, where its main prey is the mule deer. But any creature it can catch is fair game.*

During their first year, their diet of mother's milk is gradually supplemented and then replaced with morsels of wild meat. When six months old, kittens average thirty pounds (13½ kg). At some point the female leads young ones to a kill to feed; eventually she takes them on hunting trips. Weaker ones cannot cope, and die. Sometime after a year of family life, young cougars feel the urge to live alone, and mortality probably is high among those making the transition to a solitary life. Starvation is the main cause of death. But trespassing into the territory of an established male is also a grave danger.

Adult mountain lions live in fairly well-defined and exclusive home ranges, often for life, but do not seem to defend territories as do some other large predators. They appear to avoid rather than confront one another, but this is a difficult thing for biologists to ascertain. Adults do mark boundaries of home ranges with scrapes or scratchings, urine, and feces. The size of home ranges varies greatly, from reported sizes of ten to almost four hundred square miles (26–1,040 km²), depending on geography and abundance of both cats and prey.

I have been lucky enough to see a number of cougars in the wild, two of them while I was hunting elk. I saw one lion in northwestern Wyoming when the animal was stalking the same bull as I and crept silently

*Cougars hunt by a combination of stealth and short bursts of speed. At full speed, a running cougar is little more than a tawny blur in the forest.*

between the elk and myself. Some sixth sense must have warned the cat, because it looked suddenly toward where I crouched and then simply evaporated. I spotted a sleeping cougar in the Alberta Rockies with binoculars, but it also vanished when a loose rock rolled under my foot.

The mountain lion's vision is stereoscopic, meaning it can see sharp, three-dimensional images, which is ideal for hunting in daylight or darkness.

Cougars are powerful, swift sprinters—but just for fairly short distances. They can clear almost forty feet (12 meters) in one bound, and one animal, pursued by a pack of hounds, jumped vertically eighteen feet (5½ meters) into the safety of a tree.

Like most other cats, cougars have retractile claws. Other carnivores use their claws when running, but the cats use them only for gripping prey and climbing. Thus the cougar's claws, extended and withdrawn by foreleg muscles, are kept extremely sharp.

Also like all felids, or members of the world cat fam-

ily, cougars have a hyoid bone in the throat at the base of the tongue. The hyoids of the bigger cats, the lions and tigers, are composed of flexible material, enabling them to roar, but not to purr. However, the small cats (of which the cougar is the largest) have a harder hyoid; they can purr, but cannot roar. The other native North American big cat, the jaguar, *Panthera onca*, is one that roars.

### Jaguars: The Spotted Phantom
It is possible, although not absolutely certain, that jaguars no longer wander wild north of the Mexican border. But years ago they certainly were present, and maybe even locally abundant, all across the southern United States from Florida to California. Almost always loss of habitat is the reason any species completely disappears, but in the case of the jaguar, hunting for the fine spotted coat, for sport, and for livestock protection seem to be the culprits. As far as we know, the last jaguar in the United States was killed illegally in

114

Cochise County, Arizona, in 1986. It currently is a protected species.

California's last jaguar was killed near Palm Springs in 1860, at which time there may have been breeding populations as far north as the Grand Canyon and in the vicinity of present-day San Antonio, Texas. As recently as 1990, the cats were still living in the northern Mexican state of Sonora, adjacent to Arizona. But the destruction of natural forest cover all across northern Mexico is so rampant that it is doubtful if a viable population of the continent's largest cats will survive long.

Male jaguars may average more than 200 pounds (90 kg) and females about 125 pounds (56 kg), considerably larger than cougars. Adults measure up to nine feet (270 cm) from nose to tail tip. The black "spots" are really rosettes on a yellow-orange body that may blend to white on the belly.

The jaguar resembles the leopard of Asia and Africa more than any other cat, but is stockier of build with a more massive face and jaw that appears more powerful. Jaguars are good climbers, but probably are less fleet and agile than leopards or cougars.

The plain truth is that we do not know much about the life and activities of jaguars. A list of their prey in Latin America—tapirs, peccaries, capybaras, reptiles, and fish—at least suggests that they depend on camouflage and stealth rather than speed to hunt. They have always had a reputation as stock killers, and in South America more than a few have attacked and eaten humans. Like almost all cats, except African lions and cheetahs, they are solitary hunters, probably being most active at night.

A lot of folklore suggests that jaguars are animals of the night, hunting only or mainly after dark, but in Brazil's Pantanal, one of the species's last strongholds, that is not the case. The common conception that jaguars are creatures of deep, dense, green jungles also is only partly true. We now know that they also are at home in more open forests, in the lush grasslands and wetlands of South America, as well as in mountain country. Jaguars are good and willing swimmers. In the future they must become increasingly adaptable, while remaining inconspicuous, if they are to survive another century on this earth.

I have never seen a jaguar in North America nor in Mexico where an estimated one thousand may still roam; I have spotted them in Colombia and Venezu-

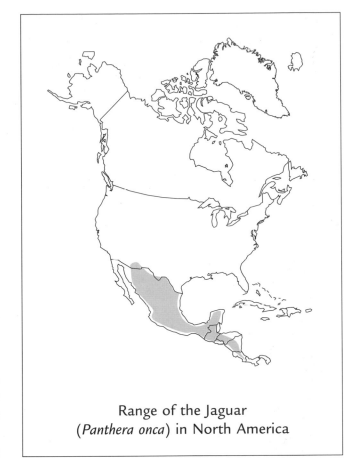

Range of the Jaguar
(*Panthera onca*) in North America

ela. Even a quick sighting is a thrill, but being close enough for long enough to focus on the yellow eyes is an indelible experience.

Nor have Peggy and I ever seen that cougar that killed the whitetail so close to our front door in Montana, although we have frequently found its tracks for almost three years. We have also found several of its other deer kills and scat defiantly left on the front lawn. Both North American big cats have a way of staying out of human view.

That may be changing somewhat. In 1994, a cougar killed a female jogger in California. In other areas where new subdivisions push farther and farther into cougar country, there have been sightings and even attacks. Cats are showing up too close for the comfort of some citizens. One cat kept strolling across the central California golf course where senior duffers from a retirement community in nearby Roseville regularly teed off. The golfers wondered if they should pack pistols along with their putters.

As the twentieth century ends, stories of a third North American big cat have been revived. According to those claiming to have seen it, the "onza" is cheetah-

like, has non-retractile claws, and attacks people without provocation, mostly in remote mountains of northern Mexico. For years it was listed in the official game regulations of Mexico and magazine articles were written about what, some said, was a cross between a cougar and a jaguar. The famous Lee brothers, hunting guides of Arizona, said they helped a client kill one in the 1930s. A prospector claimed to have seen one near Yuma. Fortunately, or unfortunately, depending on your viewpoint, this is one cat that doesn't exist and never did.

**Above:** *Although all of their actual hunting is on the ground, jaguars may use high tree perches to scan the ground below for prey.* **Left:** *Jaguars may no longer exist north of the United States–Mexico border. But reports of their existence are still occasionally heard from Texas, Arizona, and New Mexico.*

# BLACK BEAR

## *The Mighty Black Bruin*

Alex Hughes has spent most of his long life as a hunting and fishing guide in the Lake Nipissing region of Ontario. During that time he has seen his share of black bears. But one morning in June he witnessed a phase of black bear behavior he had never seen before.

While he was cooking breakfast, he spotted a dark brown female prowling around his outhouse not far away. From the light spot on one shoulder, Hughes knew it was the same sow that had visited his place the fall before with two nearly full-grown cubs. The three of them had plundered most of the apples from two trees he had planted long ago. Now the female was alone, or so the old woodsman believed, until he heard loud woofing and grunting. Suddenly two black bears larger and darker than the female arrived, fighting. Hughes put down his coffee cup and picked up his binoculars.

What Hughes saw wasn't the sparring or friendly play-fighting that he had watched in the past. These two boars were serious. They would rush one another, stand on their hind feet, box, and bite. Fur flew. Hughes later told me that the combat lasted about ten minutes before one bear, which seemed to be bleeding around an ear, finally turned and ran. Soon after that, the winner mounted the female, and the two disappeared to spend their honeymoon in the deep north woods.

Although such mating fights are probably common wherever black bears range today, they are not often observed. Next to the large cats, this species, *Ursus americanus*, is the most furtive and difficult to see in the wild of any big game animals. If not for garbage dumps, which they cannot resist, and for the total protection afforded in national parks, black bear sightings would be rare indeed.

*In early summer everywhere, black bears like this one subsist largely on the new green grass, which has a high protein content.*

There are two main reasons for this. Ever since they began to settle North America, humans have hunted bears for food, sport, hides, and simply to get rid of them. Being intelligent, bears learned to avoid their hunters—and to a bear all humans are hunters. Only the smarter ones survived to breed. In addition, black bears are strictly forest animals. They eat forest food and they need trees—large tracts of trees—for shade, refuge, and escape.

## Black Bear Characteristics

Except for wolves, no other North American big game animal exhibits as many different-colored pelts as this smallest of our native bears. Solid black is the most common, particularly in the eastern half of their range, where virtually all are entirely ebony. Moving westward, a few more dark brown, light brown, cinnamon, and rare blond bears occur. There is a slate-gray or bluish bear, called a glacier bear, living in a limited area on the southeast Alaska panhandle. A number of pure white or cream-colored animals live among the darker black bears of Princess Royal Island and the adjacent British Columbia mainland. Some dark black bears have light or whitish V-shaped patches on the chest.

When you read about them in hunting stories or newspaper articles, black bears are always described as at least "large," and occasionally as "huge." But in truth only a few ever reach great size. Cubs weigh less than a pound (½ kg) and are blind and helpless when they are born in mid-winter in a den. Their eyes open at about six weeks, and they nurse for two to three months. They will not reach full size until they are five or six years old. Adult males measure four and a half to six feet (135–180 cm) long depending on the locality. They weigh from 250 to over 400 pounds (112–180 kg), and normally are heaviest in the north. There are numerous accounts of bears reaching 600 or even 700 pounds (270–315 kg), and some of them are probably true if the animals have had steady access to human garbage heaps. Fully grown females weigh from 150 to 250 pounds (67–112 kg).

The average black bear wandering through the forest does not look like an animal that can run as fast as a racehorse. With its short claws, it can quickly scale any tree stout enough to support it, and it can swim powerfully against a strong, cold river current or across a wide lake. Altogether this is an agile, powerful, athletic animal. Years ago, as a publicity stunt in Green Bay, Wisconsin, the players of a championship high

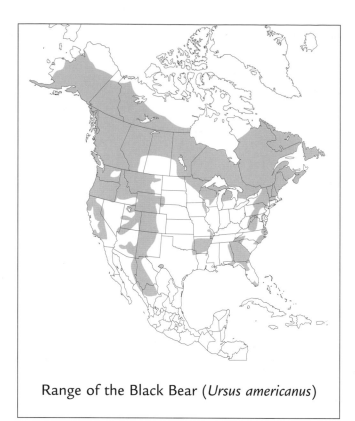

Range of the Black Bear (*Ursus americanus*)

Adult front foot length: Approximately 3¾ inches (94 mm) not including heel pad or claws
Adult front foot width: Approximately 4½ inches (112 mm)

Adult hind foot length: Approximately 7 inches (175 mm) not including claws
Adult hind foot width: Approximately 3½ inches (87 mm)

Track of the Black Bear (*Ursus americanus*)

school football team "scrimmaged" with a pet bear that was muzzled for their protection. While movie cameras rolled, the animal charged back and forth over the field and no one was ever able to catch it, let alone tackle it.

**Above:** *This brown-phase black bear is foraging around the edge of a forest pond. The bruin was later observed trying to catch frogs and ducklings.* **Left:** *Mostly a dweller of deep forests, this northern Minnesota black bear pauses before plunging in and crossing the woodland stream.*

## Black Bears Through the Seasons

When black bears emerge from hibernation in early spring, they are thin, but for a time the dark fur is thick and shiny—so shiny, in fact, that at this time bears are the most difficult to photograph properly with a film exposure that captures both the pelt and the background. There are spring bear hunting seasons where the animals are numerous enough. But adults soon begin to shed their winter coats and are not attractive until new hair fully replaces the old by late summer. During mid-summer, the bears desperately require shade during hot middays; in bright sunshine the temperature of their black pelts can reach 185°F (85°C). When an animal can no longer maintain its body temperature below 104°F (40°C) by panting or bathing, it will die.

One way that bears mark territory is by standing up and claw-marking trees. There is a heavily used deer path along Deep Creek through our own property in south-central Montana, but whitetails are not the only large mammals regularly using it. At intervals along the trail, a black bear has been clawing the trunks of quaking aspens about six feet (2 meters) above the ground for several years. I am not certain if this animal is marking a territory boundary or simply blazing and reblazing its own supply route. That trail winds through thickets of chokecherries, buffalo berries, and wild rose hips—all preferred black bear foods.

After a heavy rain one morning, I was able to measure the footprints of the Deep Creek bear that were clearly and freshly imprinted in soft mud. The hind paws were about seven inches long and four inches wide (17½x10 cm). The fore footprints measured about four inches square (10 cm²). Although shaped somewhat like a human footprint, the heel of the bear's hind feet did not show on the firmer ground.

There is an old Chippewa Indian saying that "nothing has eyes like an eagle, ears like a deer, or the nose of a bear," and that comes close to absolute fact. From our own experiences watching and photographing black bears, I would rate their vision as fair, their hearing as excellent, and their sense of smell as far beyond human comprehension. They depend on extremely sensitive noses to locate food, including food at a great distance. A bear probably conserves much energy because its nose gives an early indication of what is available for some distance all around. That way there is less need for unproductive forays.

Black bears are not social. Males are bachelors, and except for during the brief breeding season or around garbage dumps, they lead solitary lives. They use the same super scenting ability to locate the trails of females coming into heat or to track a rival boar following the same sow. Biologists believe that boar fights such as the one Alex Hughes saw are not unusual, and that sometime both the winner and loser will mate with the female.

Females nurse their one to five cubs throughout the winter, and in northern latitudes without ever leaving their dens, until spring arrives and the cubs are old enough to follow them. Rarely do more than the strongest two cubs of a litter survive. The cubs follow the mother's trail as well as her example, and she usually will fiercely defend them with claws and sharp canine teeth. Black bears, cubs and adults alike, make a variety of sounds: whining and whimpering when separated, snorting or growling softly when playing. On a number of occasions we have watched well-fed cubs playing and, although this can become rough fun, mothers never seem to intervene.

Much of every bear's life, spring through fall, is spent in the search for food. When it's abundant, they gorge during mornings and evenings, bedding in shade nearby to sleep it off. But all bears must travel more widely during times when berry, nut (especially acorn), and green crops fail, and they may be seen feeding at any time of day or night. Black bears are omnivorous opportunists and in a pinch might eat anything their stomachs can recycle. Favorite wild foods are fruits and berries, succulent grasses, forbs, and insects. A few seem to specialize in finding small game or deer fawns soon after they are born. Black bears will fish for spawning salmon in the Pacific Northwest, smelt in the Great Lakes, and suckers anywhere. They enjoy dining on such farm crops as corn and oats, orchard fruits, honey, or anything growing in rural vegetable gardens. Carrion and road-killed wildlife are relished, as is the waste from human tables at garbage dumps.

Both males and females establish territories that they defend from other bears. But because of the species's shy nature and forest habitat, it is difficult to exactly measure territories or to determine how vigor-

*Not all black bears are black, especially in the western United States and Canada. In the low summer sun, this one has a shiny reddish pelt, which it will soon shed.*

**Above:** *This black bear was photographed along the trail during a summer hike to Gunsight Pass in Glacier National Park. A split second later it disappeared.* **Right:** *Frightened at the approach of a larger bear, this cub found refuge high in a tree. All black bears are capable climbers, but younger ones are more agile and can climb higher.*

ously they are defended. There probably is a lot more trespassing and long-distance travel during years of food scarcity. And bears may be more tolerant during years of plenty. But we do know that during long periods of drought and poor wild food crops, all the bears in a certain region might migrate far in search of better conditions. In fact, there have been periodic shifts in populations from Ontario across the international boundary into Minnesota and back again, as revealed by live-capturing and tagging of the animals.

Black bears cannot honestly be regarded as dangerous animals. They have attacked a few people over the decades, usually under abnormal circumstances, and it would be foolish not to regard any nearby bear with caution. They can become a nuisance and threatening, especially when they become addicted to human foods, as they will go to great extremes to get more. By far the majority of reported incidents of bears attacking humans around campgrounds result from bears that have obtained food from campers.

## Black Bears and Grizzlies

In the Rocky Mountains from Yellowstone northward, through western Canada, and into Alaska, the bear a hiker or camper might meet may not be a black bear. Here *Ursus americanus* shares its range with, and is subordinate to, the grizzly bear. It is wise to be able to tell black bears and grizzlies apart—quickly—and that may not be easy in the dim light of morning or the dappled forest light of a sunny afternoon. It is impossible to distinguish between the two by color alone, because grizzlies also are both light and dark.

Keep these points in mind: Black bears have longer ears and longer, thinner snouts than grizzlies; grizzlies have wider, more concave faces. Viewed from the side, the grizzly has a noticeable hump above the front shoulder. I think grizzlies also have a more swaggering, confident, pigeon-toed gait than black bears. If the adult animal climbs or is already in a tree, it is definitely a black bear.

Do grizzlies and black bears get along where their ranges and territories overlap? They probably do, as they have for thousands of years, particularly in times when food is abundant. Black bears might suffer most when it is not. There is no doubt that a hungry adult of either species would snatch a cub of the other, given the chance. Grizzlies have been observed dragging away and eating black bear cubs in Waterton and Banff National Parks in Alberta, Canada.

## The Future of the Black Bear

Probably no one person has spent more time studying black bears more thoroughly or more intimately than Lynn Rogers of Ely in northern Minnesota. According to this busy, enthusiastic biologist, not only do all these animals need trees, but they also have a definite preference: white pines over all other species. During one six-year study in northeastern Minnesota, Rogers found that 90 percent of the spring beds of females with cubs were located beneath the oldest white pines, which made up less than 1 percent of all the trees in the area. One likely explanation is that both the rough bark and tough branches of white pines make them the best places for cubs to climb quickly when there is danger. This tree species also provides much shade in the hot mid-summer.

White pines are equally important, maybe even more important, to the Minnesota black bears in winter. Older trunks are often hollow near the bases and provide the only hollows of any tree species thereabouts big enough for denning. Pregnant females, especially, seem to prefer them. Such trees have become rare, however, because humans love the towering white pines that live as long as six centuries even more than do the bears. Lynn Rogers estimates that only 67,000 acres (26,800 hectares) of white pines of all ages survive in Minnesota, where about 3,500,000 acres (1,400,000 hectares) of them once covered the land. The same ratio is true from Michigan northward to Ontario. The majestic, towering evergreens were cut and are still being cut for lumber and to clear land for agriculture.

Just how scarce the white pines have become was shown in a study conducted in a section of the Boundary Waters Canoe Area Wilderness of Minnesota, which is protected from logging. Rogers found just three old-growth white pines in a two-hundred-year-old forest—and bears used all three as dens. We can only wonder what effect the relentless cutting of northern white pine forests is having, not only on the black bears, but on all other native wildlife of the region.

Because of their wariness and ability to adjust to changing land use, black bears are faring well as the twentieth century ends. They once inhabited almost all forested areas from central Mexico northward to the sub-Arctic. They still at least survive in most of this range, although in much smaller numbers, especially in the eastern and southeastern United States where early colonists found them abundant.

# GRIZZLY BEAR

## *Ruler of the North Woods*

The summer and fall of 1995 was a grim time for relations between humans and grizzly bears. Early on July 4, Marcie Trent, 77, and her son Larry Waldron, 45, both of Anchorage, Alaska, went hiking on the trail toward Rabbit Lake in Chugach State Park. They were accompanied by Trent's grandson, Art Abel, age 15. Trent was a remarkable woman, an avid runner who had covered about 70,000 miles (112,000 km) in competition and had completed some seventy marathons. But her splendid physical condition did not save her from a bear attack on the trail. Both she and Waldron were mauled and killed; Abel escaped by climbing a tree.

Apparently the hikers had come upon the bear feeding on a moose carcass, which Alaska Fish & Game biologists later found nearby. Although bears often are seen in the popular park, this was the first fatal attack there in its twenty-five-year history.

One night two months later, most of the campers in the Lake Louise campground in Alberta's Banff National Park retired early because of the cool temperatures at that high altitude. Suddenly, at about 3 A.M., there was screaming and terror as a female grizzly bear with a yearling cub went on a rampage. For no apparent reason, they tore into and through three tents in which six young women from Germany, Australia, and Montana were sleeping. All were mauled and bitten; two were hospitalized in serious condition.

Park officials were totally unable to explain the attack, because 1995 was not a year when the natural food crops of bears in Alberta had failed. All the campers had properly locked their food in the special storage bins in the campground. Park authorities had no choice but to close for the season this popular campground in the Canadian Rockies.

*Just before disappearing for the winter into hibernation, this young grizzly has found the carcass of a deer. Unfortunately, the pickings from it are slim.*

Norman Ashwood works as a carpenter in Glacier National Park. On his days off he hikes the spectacular back country with his wife, Rita. Walking on a trail near the Fifty Mountain campsite on (unlucky) September 13, he was on the ground beneath a bear almost before he knew what hit him. The pepper spray canister he usually carried was back in camp. After biting Ashwood all over, the bear wandered away. Rita half hiked, half ran twelve miles (19 km) to Granite Park Chalet to summon help. Except for the scars and trauma, Ashwood recovered and is in good health today. He remains somewhat philosophical about the incident.

At about the same time, bear-human incidents were also breaking out in the Yellowstone ecosystem. A teenager was mauled in the Beartooth Mountains. Soon after, Wyoming wildlife managers trapped and removed three grizzlies from the valley of the North Fork of the

*Above:* *A young grizzly explores the beautiful high country near Glacier National Park. Most grizzlies spend their lives roaming over spectacular, pure wilderness landscapes.* *Left: Sable Pass in Denali National Park, Alaska, is prime grizzly bear country. The authors have seen as many as seven here at one time during late August.*

Shoshone River where they were prowling around homes. The year's crop of whitebark pine nuts, a traditional grizzly food, was poor, and the hungry animals were coming down from the high country in search of food. Another grizzly that was killing cattle near Meeteetse, Wyoming, had to be trapped and moved far away. At the same time, still another grizzly attacked an elk hunter and his guide in the Thorofare region of the Shoshone National Forest. The guide was treated for wounds to his head and upper body.

Not so lucky were hunters Shane Fumerton and William Caspell, who shot a large bull elk near Radium Hot Springs, British Columbia. They were dressing out the carcass and taking the antlers when they were surprised by a female grizzly with twin yearling cubs. No one knows if the mother bear was protecting her cubs or trying to claim the meat. Provincial wildlife officer Sean Sharpe noted that "some bears in the region are so used to eating the remains left by hunters that they now associate the sound of a gun with their next meal and, with their keen sense of smell, head directly toward it." The two hunters were both mauled by the bear but have since recovered.

Bob Nichols also was taken by surprise when he was hunting near a beaver dam north of Fort St. James, British Columbia, a few days later. Nichols virtually stumbled into a female grizzly with three cubs, and she attacked him immediately. Unable even to raise his rifle, Nichols did reach his belt knife and with it kept slashing at the bear's throat and eyes as it chewed on his legs and chest. The bear backed off and slowly died from the loss of blood. Nichols was able to fire his rifle and alert his companions. They found him and carried him out of the bush on a makeshift stretcher of alder poles and coats. That ended what some bear experts consider the "mad season of '95."

## Brown and Grizzly Bears

About 40,000 years ago, the ancestors of these aggressive grizzly bears and the black ones, invaded North America from Asia via a narrow land bridge that then existed across the Bering Sea. New DNA evidence seems to show that there were several waves of migrations, with the first wave moving toward southeastern Alaska and beyond. Bears of a second wave went toward Kodiak Island. The final group traveled northeastward toward the Arctic as recently as 15,000 years ago.

Range of the Grizzly Bear (*Ursus arctos*)

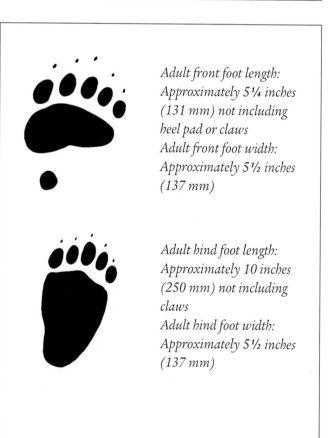

*Adult front foot length: Approximately 5¼ inches (131 mm) not including heel pad or claws*
*Adult front foot width: Approximately 5½ inches (137 mm)*

*Adult hind foot length: Approximately 10 inches (250 mm) not including claws*
*Adult hind foot width: Approximately 5½ inches (137 mm)*

Track of the Grizzly Bear (*Ursus arctos*)

*Above:* When summer blends into fall, Alaskan grizzlies such as this one begin to search for ripening berries on which they gorge themselves as long as the supply lasts. *Left:* A young grizzly is keeping its eye on its mother, grazing on fresh green grass not far away. Its survival depends on staying close to her at all times.

*Yellowstone grizzlies, perhaps siblings, erupt suddenly in an angry fight for no apparent reason. The fray ends as suddenly as it began.*

*Two heavy old male brown bears dispute a fishing territory on the McNeil River. This is the world's greatest bear watching place summer after summer.*

Biologist Lance Craighead, youngest of the well-known Craighead-Yellowstone bear studies family, notes that humans crossed the land bridge at the same time and that the two species—bears and people—really were traveling companions. Among the other animals reaching North America this way were mastodons, wolves, camels, lions, and a huge short-faced bear that was more than twice the size of our grizzlies today. All of these are gone now except the grizzlies, or brown bears, which survive pretty much unchanged. In fact, the only obstacles that stand squarely in the path of the bear's continued survival are humans and our invasion of the bears' world.

Scientists have long disagreed, and probably will continue to disagree, on the proper classification for this remarkable survivor. The consensus now is that there are two separate subspecies of *Ursus arctos*, the brown, or grizzly, bear. The first and largest, *U.a. middendorffi*, has the smallest range. It lives along the Pacific Coast from central British Columbia northwestward along the southern Alaskan coast and on many offshore islands. This subspecies also is called Kodiak, coastal, Peninsula, and marine bear; I will refer to it hereafter as the brown bear.

The other subspecies is *U.a. horribilis*, an inland bear that two centuries ago ranged widely west of the Mis-

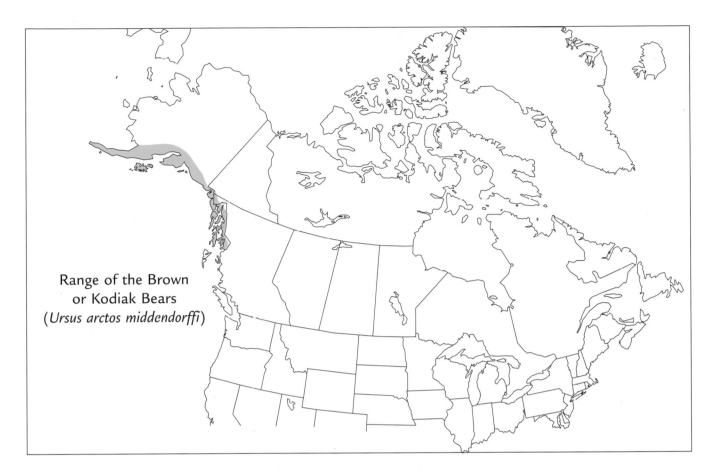

Range of the Brown
or Kodiak Bears
(*Ursus arctos middendorffi*)

*Front adult foot length:
Approximately 7 inches
(175 mm) not including
heel pad or claws
Front adult foot width:
Approximately 9 inches
(225 mm)*

*Adult hind foot length:
Approximately 16 inches
(400 mm) not including
claws
Adult hind foot width:
Approximately 10½ inches
(262 mm)*

Track of the Brown or Kodiak Bears
(*Ursus arctos middendorffi*)

sissippi River, but now lives only in more mountainous, unsettled areas from Yellowstone Park, the Bob Marshall Wilderness, and Glacier National Park north through Alberta, British Columbia, Yukon, and interior Alaska. This subspecies typically is known as the grizzly bear, sometimes called silvertip because of the light-colored tips on its dark body hair. A few of these bears, smaller in size than the brown bear, still range across northern Canada and are called Arctic, tundra, or barren ground grizzlies.

Inland grizzlies and coastal brown bears standing side by side are all but indistinguishable to anyone except those who have spent lifetimes hunting, studying, or photographing both. Both are properly classified as omnivores, but their diets probably are what most separate the two subspecies. Considering their mainly coastal habitat, it's no surprise that brown bears depend on meat, fish, and other sea creatures to a far greater extent than do inland grizzlies. Although they will eat anything that they can recycle, these grizzlies depend much more on plant foods; thus, they are slower growing. Some wild grizzlies probably live out their entire lives without ever tasting meat.

## Brown and Grizzly Bear Characteristics

Both brown and grizzly cubs are born in mid-winter dens to hibernating mothers. They weigh about a pound (½ kg) at birth, and are blind and helpless except for the vital ability to nurse.

By seven or eight years, most of these bears will reach their maximum size: about 900 or 1,000 pounds (405–450 kg) for male grizzlies, 1,600 pounds (720 kg) for male browns. But a grizzly bear that measures eight feet (240 cm) long and weighs over 600 pounds (270 kg) is a big one. So is a brown bear that reaches ten feet (300 cm) long and exceeds 800 pounds (360 kg). Females of both subspecies are on average about one-third smaller than males of the same age living in the same habitat.

All of these bears tend to be more solitary than social, although siblings age two to four or five might travel and live together. Because their food supplies often are concentrated on salmon spawning streams, many browns learn to get along together reasonably well for several weeks in summer so that all can feed on the annual salmon runs. The McNeil River State Game Reserve and Katmai National Park, both in south-central Alaska, are excellent examples of where and how concentrations of bears work out a social system or hierarchy that allows them to coexist in relative harmony. Inland grizzlies, on the other hand, are seldom tolerant of others nearby, probably because the living is a lot harder and there is no surplus food.

The diet of many if not most coastal brown bears varies little from year to year. Hibernation ends when there is enough fresh green grass on which to gorge, with the chance of finding a winter-killed caribou or blacktailed deer. A few are able to capture live fawns or calves. Most then move downslope toward the ocean's edge to dig clams, find mussels, and await the surge of spawning salmon into familiar streams. McNeil River refuge manager and record-keeper Larry Aumiller found that many bears return to this same river to resupply and grow fat every year of their lives. When the salmon bonanza ends, these bears follow old familiar trails toward ripening berry crops. Then, sleek and fat, it's back to hibernation.

Biologist Steve Gniadek recently discovered that some grizzly bears in Glacier National Park are emerging from hibernation in mid-winter, or maybe not hibernating at all. While tracking during January and February the wolves and lions now numerous in the Montana park, he often found grizzly tracks in the snow leading to and scavenging the lion and wolf kills of deer and elk. A large grizzly can chase a one-hundred-twenty-pound (54-kg) cougar or even a wolf pack from a deer carcass. It's sort of like a human raiding the refrigerator at midnight.

## The Bear's Fishing Skills

Among mine and Peggy's greatest wildlife experiences has been watching the activities of bears along salmon streams. The largest, oldest bears always stake out the best fishing spots. Mothers have the most difficult task—not only must they catch enough salmon to feed the entire family, but they must keep cubs out of trouble and away from boars that would kill them.

Not all brown bears are equally skilled at fishing. Some play the waiting game beside a river eddy, crouched and patiently waiting for a salmon to swim near before pouncing. Others have learned to snatch salmon in midair as they leap upward and over the falls. Stalking, swimming, and chasing schools of fish in shallow water are other tactics. One bear we watched was able to score by snorkeling and attacking from below. A few never "fish" at all, but intimidate other, smaller bears into dropping their fish and retreating.

Far from the streams teeming with nutritious salmon, grizzly bears must travel long distances during an average summer's day to find enough calories to support their powerful bodies' current needs in addition to providing a surplus to store as fat for the coming winter. Shortages or failures of usually reliable food crops such as blueberries and whitebark pine nuts can cause them to travel even farther than normal. During a single summer's day in Denali National Park, we watched as a grizzly female with a single cub traveled about six and a half miles (10½ km) over the tundra. Along the way she fed on grasses and succulent plants we could not identify and dug up roots and ground squirrels. Finding the squirrels seemed especially time- and energy-consuming for the amount of meat actually obtained. Grizzlies have also been observed digging marmots and pikas from their mountain dens, feed-

*A large male brown bear is finishing a salmon that it has just caught in Alaska's McNeil River.*

ing on eggs and nestlings of ground-nesting birds, tearing apart beaver lodges, and on one occasion, digging a litter of coyote pups from an underground den.

Almost whenever they meet, one subject that both bear biologists and bear hunting guides soon discuss is the intelligence of brown and grizzly bears. There usually is disagreement. The same animals that can seem to dissolve into alder or devil's club thickets, or carefully avoid the live traps of scientists who want to study them, simply cannot resist breaking into a wilderness cabin or food cache for a taste of what they smell inside. That super-keen sense of smell not only enables the animal to survive into the twenty-first century, but also gets it into deep trouble. A grizzly's hear-

ing is also excellent, but vision that can be rated only as fair may be a weak point.

## Rogue Grizzly Bears

Throughout the colorful, exciting history of settling the North American West are countless stories of rogue grizzly bears. The names of some of them—Two Toes, Old Mose, Bloody Paws, and Old Silver—as well as the names of the men who hunted them, are still part of our lore. There was Caleb Myres of Montana and Ben Lilly of New Mexico, the Old Rough Rider Teddy Roosevelt, and Kit Carson. Organized fights between bears and bull cattle were regular, bloody weekend and holiday events in frontier and gold rush towns during

are ridiculously high, hazardous waste dumps, poor air quality, and similar causes that take a much greater toll every day. Even honey bees, "gentle" riding horses, "pet" whitetailed deer, and family dogs have been far more dangerous over time.

When we are out hiking, backpacking, or photographing any wildlife, we always are alert for grizzlies because the potential for trouble certainly is present. But there basically are two kinds of wilderness areas left on the continent: those with grizzlies or brown bears and those without. It is always much more exhilarating to wander where the bears still live.

As I finish this book, there is ominous news for the grizzlies remaining in the lower forty-eight states and southern Canada, and the threat comes from an unexpected direction. In 1910, an exotic European fungus called blister rust was found on the Pacific Coast. Since then it has slowly, inexorably moved eastward into the Rocky Mountains. To date it has decimated almost half the whitebark pine tree stands in grizzly country, and that is a serious blow to the bears. As the pine nut crops fail, we may see more bears getting into trouble when they seek food elsewhere. Only time will reveal the total impact on a great game animal.

the early 1800s. One unusual man, John Capen Adams, the original "Grizzly Adams," was able to train grizzlies well enough that they followed him walking on San Francisco streets in 1856. But from the beginning, most legends and stories have been about grizzlies as villains, killers of our cattle and of us. In Montana, where Peggy and I live, strong sentiment still exists that the endangered bears are too dangerous and we would be better off and safer without them.

The truth, though, is that grizzlies are known to have killed only twenty people in the lower forty-eight United States during the past one hundred years. Contrast that to the carnage from drunken driving, pesticides, homicides, industrial accidents, speed limits that

*Above:* Pink, or humpback, salmon making a spawning run in a southwestern Alaskan stream are certain to attract bears eager to cash in on the bonanza nature has provided. *Left:* A mother brown bear surveys the swift, cold current for some sign of spawning salmon while her triplet cubs, about eighteen months old, wait hungrily nearby.

137

# POLAR BEAR

## *Ice Bear of the Arctic*

LaPerouse Bay is a shallow inlet near Cape Churchill on the western shore of Hudson Bay. Late every fall, the great white bears gather in this area. They have spent the summer inland, north of the treeline in northern Manitoba, barely subsisting on grass, berries, and nesting birds, but mostly taking life easy. The polar bears are somewhat thin and eager to get out onto Hudson Bay, which is just now beginning to freeze. Here they will spend the long, dark winter hunting seals.

One of the first places to freeze over is right here near Cape Churchill, hence the unusual concentration of bears. For a week Peggy and I "camped" here, living and traveling in a tundra buggy, an all-terrain vehicle with giant rubber-tired wheels that roll easily over the tundra. Not unlike a railroad sleeping car, it is a comfortable and convenient way to watch and photograph these splendid animals. But I couldn't escape a feeling of guilt: Not too long ago, watching these bears meant a rigorous expedition by dog sled and tenting to a bleak, bitterly cold land where the wind rarely stops blowing. By contrast, the tundra buggy seemed too easy.

There were usually about twenty bears on hand during our adventure. Most were adult males. Some spent the days and nights around us sleeping on the ice or in snow banks. Others never stopped walking. Mothers with cubs kept the young a safe distance from large males. When they met, younger males often would interrupt their day's walking to spar and scuffle until they tired of the game. Two bears went swimming in a slush hole and "dried off" by rolling in a snow drift. We saw another eating kelp that summer winds months before had washed up onto the shore. Altogether it was a remarkable opportunity to see these animals in what is certainly the world's best polar bear viewing area.

*Polar bears roam the far Arctic regions of the world. This one checks out the photographer shooting from the security of a tundra buggy.*

## Polar Bear Characteristics

The polar bear is a citizen of the world. It does not recognize national boundaries and may be found anywhere around the top of the world where seals emerge to breathe through breaks in the polar ice cap. Closely related to brown bears, *Ursus* (and until recently, *Thalarctos*) *maritimus* evolved between 50,000 and 100,000 years ago with hair color, hunting ability, and teeth ideal for living in polar regions.

By weight the ice bear is the largest land mammal living in North America. Mature males measure from eight to more than ten feet long (240–300 cm) and weigh from 900 to 1,500 pounds (405–675 kg). A few may reach a ton (900 kg) or more. Females generally weigh about 30 percent less. Both sexes have long necks and long sharp claws, the latter for gripping ice and prey. Pursuing bears by helicopter to tranquilize and examine them, pilots report that the animals can run twenty-five miles per hour (40 km/h) on glare ice or rough ground.

Based on the Boone and Crockett Club's system for measuring and rating big game animals, which relies on skull dimensions and not body size or weight, the largest known polar bear was a male taken near Kotzebue, Alaska. In fact, nearly all of the largest animals of which there is an accurate record were taken during the early 1960s on the ice off northwestern Alaska when hunting by aircraft was permitted there. Measured in another way, polar bears are twice as big as lions or tigers, the world's largest cats. Standing erect, a fully grown bear could easily look an African elephant in the eye.

It is difficult to believe that polar bears are loners by nature after watching them at Cape Churchill at least tolerating one another. But once they move out onto the ice, all go their separate ways except mothers with cubs and possibly pairs of young siblings on their own after two and a half years. Interestingly, when a mother bear captures a seal, she devours only the blubber, leaving for the youngsters the meat that contains the protein the cubs need for growth.

Exactly where the bears travel depends on their excellent eyesight and hearing, but even more on a phenomenal sense of smell. Russian scientists report that polar bears can smell dead seals from ten miles (16 km) away and that several bears from as far as fifteen miles (24 km) away soon gathered at the carcass of a dead whale. It is believed that they can hear seals swimming under the ice beneath them.

Range of the Polar Bear
(*Ursus maritimus*) in North America

*Adult front foot length: Approximately 12 inches (300 mm) not including heel pad*
*Adult front foot width: Approximately 9 inches (225 mm)*

*Adult hind foot length: Approximately 18 inches (450 mm)*
*Adult hind foot width: Approximately 11 inches (275 mm)*

Track of the Polar Bear (*Ursus maritimus*)

*In summer, a mother with half-grown cubs scavenges along the Hudson Bay shoreline. For these three, unlike other bear species, summer is never a time of plenty.*

Native people everywhere in the Arctic learned that they could bait or attract bears from long distances simply by boiling seal or whale oil and allowing the scent to drift away on the wind. One hunter shot a moose south of Churchill, Manitoba, but could not return to dress out the carcass for a few days. When he did, he found the moose had been eaten by a bear. Out of curiosity, the hunter backtracked the bear over the snowy landscape and found that it had walked almost thirty miles (48 km) in a straight line to the moose carcass— and at least part of the trip was during the dark of night.

Although its eyes are smaller than a human's— which is surprising for a creature so much larger than us—it has much better vision in all kinds of light, especially after dark. A traveling polar bear does not have to worry about obstacles in its path and can plow ahead in what for people is total darkness.

Since some days in the polar bear's world of ice and snow are dazzlingly bright, nature has equipped the species with natural sunglasses to prevent snow-blindness. A special eyelid protects the eyes from intense glare by acting as a polarizing lens.

Strange as it may seem, a polar bear's hair is shorter and not as dense as that of brown, grizzly, or black bears. When the animal is swimming, its fur has little insulating value and it is a layer of blubber that keeps the bear from freezing. The water-repellent guard hairs shed water easily and, when the bear shakes like a wet dog, the water sprays off almost completely.

Stranger still is that the hair is not really white, as a U.S. Army researcher discovered using an electron-scanning microscope. Instead it is colorless and without pigment, growing out of a black skin. It is the hair's silky surface that reflects light in such a way that it appears to be white most of the time. When the Arctic sun rises and sets, as we saw in our camera viewfinders at Cape Churchill, the color of a polar bear can change from pale yellow to gold to rose to white and back again. It is a beautiful transformation in a beautiful, wild place that all outdoorspeople should see for themselves someday.

## The Great White Hunter

In early spring, after a winter of hunting and gorging, male bears begin the search for females coming into estrus. This search may require traveling over great expanses of frozen land, even swimming from ice floe to ice floe, all the while using scent to determine the proper direction. Breeding battles between males, rarely witnessed by humans, must be savage. Many bears shot by hunters or tranquilized by scientists are badly scarred on the face and shoulders.

There is much more to be learned about how polar bears live. We know that most wander far on foot, swimming when necessary. Some may ride on ice floes for hundreds of miles. But always they must stay within reach or near the edge of open water, because this is where they will find seals and walruses, which they capture in different ways.

In May 1992, U.S. federal biologists captured a fe-

*Above: This is the western shore of Hudson Bay, Manitoba, in late November. New ice is just forming along the lonely coast. The two bears are awaiting complete freezeup so that they can begin the winter's hunting across the ice pack.* **Right:** *On a warm summer day near Cape Churchill, Manitoba, a mother polar bear rests with cubs that will soon wander away to lead lives of their own.*

male bear within sight of the oil fields at Prudhoe Bay, Alaska, and attached radio collar number 20365 around her neck. She was one of one hundred fifty polar bears tagged and released in the region. Within two and a half months, the female had logged 1,600 miles (2,560 km) of travel, roaming over Canada's Ellesmere Island, finally denning in Greenland where batteries on the radio collar gave out. It was an extraordinary and unusual odyssey, even for the white bear.

If there is a suggestion of clumsiness or sluggishness in the pigeon-toed way a bear walks, it disappears immediately when the animal begins seriously hunting. Whenever a seal hauls out near a crack in the ice, the bear begins an almost snakelike stalk. It crouches

low, chin on the ice, and slides forward silently on its belly toward the napping seal. Whenever the seal wakes up, the bear pauses and waits utterly motionless until the seal dozes again. When it is near enough for a final rush, the bear is suddenly on its feet and running. With feet as big as dinner plates and three-inch-long (7½-cm) claws, it can easily and quickly kill a five-hundred-pound (225 kg) bearded seal.

A native hunter of Eskimo Point, Northwest Territory, described to me another way that polar bears sometimes capture seals. While the seal sleeps right on the edge of the ice, the bear slowly lowers itself rump first into the water. Then after swimming either underwater or near the surface with only its nose above water, the bear suddenly lunges up and out of the water onto its next hot meal.

Canadian biologist Ian Stirling has devoted much of his career to studying polar bears, and perhaps no one else has ever spent as much time observing them. During one series of studies, watching from a promontory high above the Arctic ice of Gascoyne Inlet, Keewatin, Stirling noted that the bears here preferred not to stalk or swim after seals, but to lie perfectly still beside a seal's breathing hole in the ice, and when the unsuspecting seal surfaced, the polar bear simply grabbed it. Stirling has also seen bears walk directly and nonchalantly upwind, in full sight of hauled out seals. Then in a few sudden bounds, the bear has its

*Meeting on the newly formed ice, two young polar bears seem to be celebrating the rosy dawn by dancing. But more likely they're just sizing one another up.*

*The warm color belies the low temperature of an Arctic morning in November. These bears are searching for openings in the ice where seals haul out.*

prey and is crushing the seal's skull in its powerful jaws.

There are reports from eighteenth century explorers of polar bears catching salmon in Labrador, and they may still fish on Northwest Territory rivers where Arctic char swarm in the brief summer. No doubt they feast on belugas or white whales when the whales become stranded in pack ice and are sealed off from escape into open water. Polar bears might in turn be caught and eaten by pods of orcas, or killer whales, as they swim the Arctic Ocean edges. Biologists in Greenland have found instances where polar bears apparently killed and ate muskoxen, although they had usually ignored them. The walrus, especially the large, tusked male, may sometimes be more than a hungry polar bear can handle.

Polar bears have been seen hunting lemmings and mice. Like other bears, they cannot resist garbage and human foods. One female trailing three yearling cubs in the Churchill area seemed to spend a lot of time looking for the nests of blue geese, plovers, and other shorebirds. One of her cubs closely followed her example. But probably everything is incidental in the ice bear's diet, except seals.

## The White Bear's Future

Are polar bears dangerous to humans? Even today, in these times of snowmobiles replacing sleds and sled dogs and modern rifles replacing spears, there are few

*During a normal lifetime, a polar bear will walk over countless miles of Arctic ice and swim many miles in the icy waters of the polar regions to subsist mainly on meals of rich, meaty seals.*

remote native villages and outposts across the Arctic without at least one old resident—usually an old seal, whale, or bear hunter—who carries the scars of a polar bear incident. One thin old-timer at Pangnirtung, Baffin Island, showed us the scars on his body that he sustained when trying to drive away the bear that was killing his sled dogs. It might have killed him too, except for a friend who heard the commotion and shot the bear.

Long ago, primitive hunters could cope with the bears and vice versa, and the bears probably were less fearful of people than they have become during the last century or so of serious hunting for fur and sport. Most biologists who have worked with polar bears believe that the animals now tend to avoid people more than in the past.

What the bears cannot avoid, however, are the levels of hydrocarbons such as Dieldrin, Endrin, and DDT, and other ocean pollutants found in bear bodies that have been examined during the past twenty years. This is another case of a wild species, a splendid big game animal, sounding a wake-up call for all of us that all is far from well in our—in the world's—environment.

# A LAST WORD

Compared to wild creatures elsewhere around the world, most of the big game species of North America are in fairly good shape, with a secure future, if we do not encroach farther into our remaining wilderness and destroy their—and our—environment. But there are some danger signals we should not overlook.

Whitetail numbers are at a historic high. Yet an outbreak of epizootic hemorrhagic disease killed at least three thousand of them in eastern Wyoming and the Black Hills region late in 1995. A prolonged spell of hot, dry weather concentrated the animals around the stock ponds and other water sources where the gnats that spread the viral disease hatch in great numbers. Once infected, the Wyoming deer became lethargic and finally died of internal bleeding and organ damage. In response to the outbreak, the Wyoming Game & Fish Department canceled the whitetail hunting season and refunded permit money to about 4,800 permit holders in the area—an unprecedented move.

Of course, this could only be an isolated case and possibly was a natural reduction of a deer herd too large for its range to support. But at least a few biologists are worried and believe it could become widespread, because there are too many whitetails in too many other localities. Apparently the viral disease does not affect mule deer.

*This bighorn ram has won the annual fall tournament as the most powerful of his peers. Now he approaches a ewe coming into estrus; and a brisk chase will follow.*

Consider another example in exquisitely beautiful British Columbia, where all but a few of the animals in this book live. One-fourth of all the original temperate, coastal rain forest in the world was in this province. But already about 40 percent has been completely logged, and half the rest of it has been invaded by roads so that even more clear cutting cannot be far off. Only about 6 percent of the original old-growth rain forest is truly protected by provincial or federal government. As a result of aggressive logging practices, salmon eggs have been smothered by silt washing from cuts above rivers and the 1995 salmon runs were the lowest in memory. Coastal communities that depend almost exclusively on the fishery have been devastated. The deadly pollutants from numerous pulp mills are discharged into the waterways and have accumulated in marine life, creating ecological dead zones, which are a growing threat to bears as well as people. Just this sort of thing has led to massive species extinction elsewhere on earth. It is sobering to think that this goes on in Canada, not a Third World country that knows no better or has no other options.

Today's politicians would allow the same devastation in Alaska. Sportspeople—all of us—need to be watchful for schemes such as the one that would permit drilling for oil in Kachemak Bay, Alaska, an ex-

*Above:* Red foxes live in big game country from coast to coast on this continent. They are seldom easily observed, but their tracks are visible from sea level to many alpine meadows.
*Right:* Buffaloes trudge past steaming geysers in Yellowstone, in search of coarse grass the lies beneath the snow along the Firehole River.

tremely sensitive area for brown bears.

Early in this book I wrote that bighorn sheep once were fairly well distributed in western North America. There may have been as many as two million. Today they exist in scattered bands, exact number unknown, and not all of these are holding their own. Typical is the Big Creek drainage herd of central Idaho where, in 1995, a rapid population decline was clearly underway. University of Idaho researchers are frantically trying to learn why few lambs were being born and why so few were surviving. Their efforts are focusing on poor nutrition, stress, and disease contracted from domestic livestock. If and when they find an answer, credit must also go to Wildlife Forever, a non-profit conser-

vation arm of the North American Hunting Club, and the Foundation for North American Wild Sheep, which financed this vital study.

The work of such citizen conservation groups as these cannot be overestimated. Since 1987, Wildlife Forever has helped fund over two hundred fifty projects in forty-four states and Canadian provinces to preserve our wild heritage, according to Executive Director Douglas H. Grann.

In 1994, another new wildlife conservation group, The Mule Deer Foundation, was formed—and none too soon. For the past quarter century or so, mule deer numbers have been in a slow but steady decline. What are the problems that Foundation members plan to rectify? Most important is that range management policies on both public and private lands are not in the best interest of these browsing animals. Mule deer winter range has declined due to human encroachment. Prolonged periods of drought have been a problem. And strange as it may seem, prevention of range and forest fires for far too long has allowed many important mule deer browse plants to grow beyond edible size and has not encouraged new growth.

These are just a few of the problems that face the big game animals of North America. How well, how wisely, and how quickly we cope with them will determine how long these magnificent creatures survive.

# TROPHY HUNTING
# WITH A CAMERA

Late on a cold afternoon in the early 1950s, with a heavy snow falling, I drove slowly along Plum Brook in northern Ohio with my friend, Bill Hendershot. The state's deer hunting season had closed the day before, and neither of us had bagged the buck we had dreamed about and planned for since late summer. Now we were heading home and already planning for next year. That's when Bill nudged me with an elbow and pointed toward a patch of dense vegetation on our left.

There, staring at us from the edge of the thicket, stood a ghost with heavy antlers, the largest whitetail buck I had ever seen until that instant.

Despite a terrible attack of buck fever, I managed to roll down the car window, aim my Hasselblad camera, and snap a single photo before the animal bounded away into the snowy background, as whitetails always seem to do. Later, I had an enlarged print made from my black-and-white negative, and it was published in *Outdoor Life* magazine. Probably more than anything else, that one brief moment and that single photograph were the beginning of the rest of my life as a serious, incorrigible, unrepentant big game cameraman. There is simply no other sport, vocation, avocation, or pastime to match wildlife photography for both thrills and satisfaction. Nothing.

Consider these advantages and rewards: Trophy hunters shooting only with cameras do not have to buy expensive licenses or trust the luck of the draw for special permits. They do not worry about open or closed seasons, and in fact can hunt the year around, close to home, all across the continent, and throughout the world. Like gun hunters, they can go stalking game alone, with their families, or with old buddies. It's also great competition. There are no bag limits; you can "shoot" one trophy and then legally go looking for a still-bigger one. And another.

*Once black bears were abundant and widespread in America's Southeast. But this one is a rare—and suspicious survivor in northern Florida.*

*Above:* This one black-and-white photo of a whitetailed buck, shot during a northern Ohio snowstorm, may have been most responsible for launching a long, happy, eventful, and rewarding career as a nature/wildlife photographer. *Right:* There are few riparian areas in North America that lack some sign of raccoons. They are especially numerous in southern whitetail country.

But maybe the greatest reward of any trophy hunting is not in the mounted head on the wall or the photos in an album. Instead, it is enjoying big game country, being out in the most beautiful wild places left in North America and far beyond. The possibilities for adventure are unlimited.

One memorable trip in late August, forty years after shooting that whitetail buck in the snow, offers just one more fine example.

Peggy and I were making a float trip down the Alsek and Tatshenshini rivers from Kluane National Park, Yukon, to tidewater at remote Dry Bay, Alaska. These rivers race through one of the largest unspoiled wildernesses left on earth. During our twelve-day float we were able to "hunt" the grizzly bears and moose we passed along the way. Some of the bears strolled close to our overnight camps. So did wolves. But the highlight was our climb onto Goatherd Mountain, which is the northernmost limit of all mountain goat range. Some record-book billies are said to live on these steep slopes, which overlook great icefields.

We did not find any that we felt were record size, but through telephoto lenses we looked up and down on handsome goats living in a magnificent landscape high above clouds, glaciers, total wilderness, and a turbulent river. The pictures of them will always remind us of a remarkable day.

There are two kinds of big game trophy hunting with a camera. For the first, and by far the most difficult, you go out exactly as if hunting with a bow or firearm in open hunting country. For the second, you hunt only in national, provincial, and state parks where gunning is not permitted and where the animals are much easier to approach. Most of our photos in this book were made in these sanctuaries, which are open to everyone.

I greatly admire any photographer who chooses to hunt the first, or more difficult way, because it is necessary to approach much more closely with a camera than with a rifle to score. But even on many national park lands, getting near enough to the top trophies can be a considerable challenge, requiring both patience and knowledge of the animal's lifestyle, and especially of its tolerance of humans. It's important to know about or read about the game before going out with photo gear in hand.

Fortunately, modern photographic gear makes the game much easier. The best, if not the only cameras to use, are 35mm single lens reflex (SLRs) cameras, which are light, reliable, easy to handle, with many automatic features such as motor drives, autofocus, and auto-rewind. Best of all, today's 35mm cameras and telephoto lenses combine to permit shooting trophies from some distance away, much farther than was possible a few decades ago.

The telephoto lenses we have used most of the time are 400mm (or eight power) or 600mm (or twelve power). With such heavy, bulky optical equipment, it is necessary to mount camera and telephoto lens on an adjustable tripod with a smooth-panning, quick-release tripod head such as the Wimberley. Of course, all of this is heavy to carry far and becomes heavier as the carrier grows older. But I have often noticed that my gear is much lighter on those trips when the deer or bears or bighorns are sharp and almost filling my viewfinder in bright sunlight. Also, the gear we use today has autofocus capability and that is a tremendous boon when animals are in motion or when the photographer's vision is no longer 20/20.

When we are in the field, and likely to wander far from our small camper van, which is a base camp wherever it's parked, we also carry shorter lenses for shooting landscapes and habitat pictures, extra rolls of film, filters, light foul-weather gear to cover both ourselves and our cameras, insect repellent, high-energy snacks, and a canteen of water in light backpacks. On good days, this extra burden weighs almost nothing at all.

Like many, if not most, wildlife photographers today, we feel a special sense of urgency to get out there and shoot.

# ORGANIZATIONS

Boone and Crockett Club
Old Milwaukee Depot
250 Station Drive
Missoula, MT 59801
(406) 542-1888

Canadian Nature Federation
1 Nicholas Street, Suite 520
Ottawa, Ontario
KIN 7B7 Canada
(613) 562-3447

Foundation For North American
Big Game
P.O. Box 2710
Woodbridge, VA 22192

Foundation For North American
Wild Sheep
720 Allen Avenue
Cody, WY 82414
(307) 527-6261

Great Bear Foundation
P.O. Box 1289
Bozeman, MT 59771
(406) 586-5533

Greater Yellowstone Coalition
13 South Willson Avenue
Bozeman, MT 59771
(406) 586-1593

KOA Kampgrounds Of America
P.O. Box 30558
Billings, MT 59114
(406) 248-7444

The Mule Deer Foundation
1005 Terminal Way, Suite 140
Reno, NV 89502
(800) 344-BUCK

National Wildlife Federation
8925 Leesburg Pike
Vienna, VA 22184

North American Hunting Club
P.O. Box 3401
Minneapolis, MN 55343
(800) 922-4868

Rocky Mountain Elk Foundation
2291 West Broadway
P.O. Box 8249
Missoula, MT 59807-8249

Safari Club International
4800 W. Gates Pass Road
Tucson, AZ 85745

Whitetails Unlimited
1715 Rhode Island Street
Sturgeon Bay, WI 54235
(800) 743-6777

Wildlife Forever
12301 Whitewater Drive, Suite 210
Minnetonka, MN 55343
(612) 936-0605

Wilderness Society
900 17th Street NW
Washington, D.C. 20006-2596
(202) 833-2300

Wimberley Design
133 Bryarly Road
Winchester, VA 22603
(540) 665-2744

# REFERENCES AND SUGGESTED READING

Bauer, Erwin. *Bears in Their World.* New York: Outdoor Life Books, 1990.

Bauer, Erwin. *Horned and Antlered Game.* New York: Outdoor Life Books, 1986.

Bauer, Erwin. *Predators of North America.* New York: Outdoor Life Books, 1988.

Bauer, Erwin. *Wild Alaska.* New York: Outdoor Life Books, 1988.

Bauer, Erwin, and Peggy Bauer. *Antlers: Nature's Majestic Crown.* Stillwater, MN: Voyageur Press, 1995.

Bauer, Erwin, and Peggy Bauer. *Bears: Behavior, Ecology, Conservation.* Stillwater, MN: Voyageur Press, 1996.

Bauer, Erwin, and Peggy Bauer. *Mule Deer: Behavior, Ecology, Conservation.* Stillwater, MN: Voyageur Press, 1995.

Bauer, Erwin, and Peggy Bauer. *Whitetails: Behavior, Ecology, Conservation.* Stillwater, MN: Voyageur Press, 1993.

Bauer, Erwin, and Peggy Bauer. *Yellowstone.* Stillwater, MN: Voyageur Press, 1993.

Brakefield, Tom. *Kingdom of Might: The World's Big Cats.* Stillwater, MN: Voyageur Press, 1993

Brummer, Fred. *Arctic Animals: A Celebration of Survival.* Toronto: McClelland and Stewart, Ltd., 1986.

Calif, George. *Caribou and the Barren Lands.* Toronto: Firefly Books, 1981.

Chadwick, Douglas. *A Beast the Color of Winter.* San Francisco: Sierra Club Books, 1983.

Clark, James L. *The Great Arc of the Wild Sheep.* Norman, OK: University of Oklahoma Press, 1964.

Dalrymple, Byron. *North American Big-Game Animals.* New York: Outdoor Life Books, 1978.

Davids, Richard C., and Dan Guravich. *Lords of the Arctic: A Journey Among the Polar Bears.* New York: Macmillan, 1982.

Domico, Terry. *Bears of the World.* New York: Facts on File, 1988.

Gerlach, Duane, ed. *Deer.* Mechanicsburg, PA: Stackpole Books, 1994.

King, Judith. *Seals of the World.* 2nd ed. British Museum. London: Oxford University Press, 1983.

Laycock, George. *The Wild Bears.* New York: Outdoor Life Books, 1986.

Ricciuti, Edward. *The Natural History of North America.* New York: Gallery Books, 1990.

Rocky Mountain Elk Foundation. *Majesty: Visions From the Heart of Elk Country.* Helena, MT: Falcon Press, 1993.

Watson, Lyall. *Sea Guide to Whales of the World.* New York: Elsevier-Dutton, 1981.

Russell, Charles. *Spirit Bear: Encounters With the White Bear of the Western Rainforest.* Toronto: Key Porter Books, 1994.

Walker, Tom. *River of Bears.* Stillwater, MN: Voyageur Press, 1993.

Whitehead, G. Kenneth. *The Whitehead Encyclopedia of Deer.* Stillwater, MN: Voyageur Press, 1993.

Wildlife Management Institute. *Big Game of North America Ecology and Management.* Harrisburg, PA: Stackpole Books, 1978.

# INDEX

158

# ABOUT THE AUTHORS

*Simply stated, here is the luckiest fellow on earth. Not too many others have been able to photograph the wild world and its wild creatures, almost daily for over a half century.*

*Probably the best, surely the nicest and most determined, female wildlife photographer in the world. Many of the bears, sheep, and whitetailed deer in this book are her old friends.*

Erwin and Peggy Bauer are among the world's most published photographers and writers on travel, adventure, and environmental subjects. Based in Paradise Valley, Montana, the Bauers have specialized in photographing wildlife worldwide for over forty years. Their images come from the Arctic to the Antarctic, Borneo to Brazil, Africa to India, Madagascar to Malaysia, and beyond. The couple has won many awards for wildlife photography in national and international photography competitions.

Erwin and Peggy Bauer's recent magazine credits include *Natural History, Outdoor Life, Audubon, National Geographic, Smithsonian, Wildlife Conservation, National Wildlife* and *International Wildlife, Sierra, Safari, Chevron USA,* and *The Nature Conservancy.* Their photographs annually illustrate the calendars of Voyageur Press, the Sierra Club, the Audubon Society, World Wildlife Fund, and others.

The Bauers have more than a dozen books currently in print, including *Yellowstone; Whitetails: Behavior, Ecology, Conservation; Antlers: Nature's Majestic Crown; Mule Deer: Behavior, Ecology, Conservation; Elk: Behavior, Ecology, Conservation;* and *Bears: Behavior, Ecology, Conservation,* all published by Voyageur Press.